Andreza Silva

(469) 831 11 07

A Teachers' Grammar

An Approach to the Central Problems of English

R. A. Close

Introduction and
Commentary by Michael Lewis

THOMSON

HEINLE

Australia Canada Mexico Singapore Spain United Kingdom United States

THOMSON
HEINLE

A Teachers' Grammar
The Central Problems of English
R.A. Close

Publisher/Global ELT: *Christopher Wenger*
Executive Marketing Manager, Global ELT/ESL: *Amy Mabley*

Printed in the UK.
  2 3 4 5 6 7 8 9 10   06 05 04 03 02

For more information contact Heinle, 25 Thomson Place, Boston, MA 02210 USA,
or you can visit our Internet site at http://www.heinle.com

ISBN: 0 906717 48 5

Acknowledgments

It was Sir Stanley Unwin, famous head of a distinguished publishing house, who first insisted that this
book be published under the title *English as a Foreign Language*. When it appeared in print, he
expressed his satisfaction in the words: "This will be revised by my successors and yours". Sir Stanley
died in 1968, aged 83. Dedicating this version to his memory, I take this opportunity of expressing my
gratitude not only to his successors who helped me prepare the second and third editions but also to Mr
Michael Lewis of Language Teaching Publications who insisted that the book should be kept alive in a
more up-to-date form.
R.A.C. 1992

The Author

R.A. Close began formulating his view of English grammar when teaching in China from 1933 to 1938.
He joined the British Council and developed his ideas in Greece, Chile, Czechoslovakia and Japan.
Returning in 1968, he was appointed Honorary Research Fellow, University College London, where he
assisted in the production of major grammars of contemporary English.

CONTENTS

This book appeared in its first edition 30 years ago, from an academic rather than a language teaching publisher. It was a landmark of its time, and praise was lavished upon it by many, if not most, contemporary grammarians.

This new, revised edition retains all the insight and clarity of the original text, but has been slightly up-dated in terms of content and re-designed to make the book easier to read.

It is unusual among grammar books, in that it has been written so that, rather than being used only for reference, its chapters can be read. Each chapter represents a coherent, and developing argument, exemplified by reference to an enormous number of examples. For native speakers of English, it provides an invaluable and clear insight into the way of looking at English which is essential if the material is to be presented to someone whose native language is not English. Native speakers simply do not think of the Primary Distinctions which the author introduces in chapter 2, but it is these distinctions which underlie many of the grammatical choices which are intrinsic to English. For the non-native speaker, the book provides a wealth of detailed information and examples, but more importantly demonstrates some of the hierarchically more important distinctions of English, and shows how these fundamental distinctions re-occur in different disguises in quite different parts of the grammatical system. The author constantly has in mind the importance of a coherent over-view of grammar.

Three features of the book remain outstanding contributions to the understanding of English grammar for both native and non-native speakers:

1. The author shows clearly that grammar is more than a mass of detail, and that certain Primary Distinctions of thought provide a coherence and system which many other approaches to grammar fail to develop. Seeing grammar from this point of view is intellectually satisfying, practically reassuring, and seems to have radical implications for the way grammar might be presented in text books and classrooms.

2. The author's presentation of the verb system shows a clear, coherent over-view. Instead of a seemingly endless string of tenses, the author shows that a simple set of symmetric contrasts ensures that the English verb system is simple, regular and, again, much more easily understood than many grammatical presentations would suggest.

On a personal note, I would add that reading this book some years ago was the inspiration for my own attempt to understand the English verb as a coherent whole, which ultimately resulted in publication of *The English Verb, LTP, 1986.*

3. Much grammar is a matter of **fact** – we say *children*, not *childs*, *bought* not *buyed;* and the learner needs to choose between 'right' and 'wrong' language. That matter is, of course, well known to all teachers and learners. One of the most remarkable features of this book, however, is the author's introduction of the idea of **Grammar as Choice**, where the language user has a choice between two possible 'right' sentences, in the sense of grammatically well-formed, but where each has a slightly different meaning – *We stopped in/at London for two hours; I live/am living in Powell Road.* The distinction between objective Grammar as Fact, and subjective Grammar as Choice is, I think, the author's own original, and very powerful insight. Its importance reappears numerous times throughout the book.

It has been a great pleasure to prepare this new revised edition. It is a book which profoundly influenced me, and I am delighted that it will now be available to a new generation of readers. Read it carefully and with reflection, and it will reward you with an understanding that English is simpler, more logical and systematic, and in that intellectually satisfying sense, more beautiful than may have been apparent to you before.

Michael Lewis

Hove, 1992

1   Rules in English Grammar

HAS ENGLISH A GRAMMAR?

It has often been said that English has no grammar, or that, if it has, there are no rules in it. English has indeed very few of the kind of inflections, on the end of nouns and verbs, that play such an important part in the grammar of many other languages. English adjectives have no inflections at all, apart from the -er and -est of short words like *longer* and *longest*. We can accurately predict the whole 'conjugation' of every verb in modern English from a small set of rules and a fixed list of irregularities. Nor has English grammar a place for gender in nouns. *Cow* is not 'feminine gender' as opposed to the 'masculine' *bull*. *Cow* and *bull* are two separate words, one referring to a female of a species of animal, the other to the male. Both words can be preceded by a set of determiners, such as *a, any, each, either, every, my, the, this, that*, each of which has one form only.

English grammar is chiefly a system of syntax that decides the order and patterns in which words are arranged in sentences. The system works largely with the help of what are called grammatical or structural words – auxiliary verbs, determiners, pronouns, prepositions and conjunctions. These words form a 'closed set', i.e. there is a fixed number of them and new members are not admitted.

It is also true that English grammar has no rules established for it by any authority. Individual grammarians have stated their own opinions and preferences and have made up their own body of rules. According to present-day thinking there are rules in English grammar that can be accurately formulated from the observation and analysis of a large number of examples of widely accepted educated usage. The rules so formulated can account for the way in which competent users of the language produce original acceptable utterances, sentences, speeches and written texts.

GRAMMAR AS FACT

English grammar is first and foremost a matter of fact. We say *one man, two men; write, wrote, written; he may drive, he wants to drive, no one will stop him driving*. Whoever learns English must accept such forms and constructions as facts, and must develop the habit of using them in appropriate situations. Helping us to observe and remember the facts, the linguist arranges them methodically and, where possible, draws general rules from them, perhaps explaining historically how they came to be what they are. But the facts remain, decided for us. *Men* or *I wrote* or *he wants to* is 'right'; **mans, *I writed, *he mays to* are 'wrong'; there we have no choice.

GRAMMAR AS CHOICE

Often in speaking and writing English we have a choice of forms, each of which by itself is correct. *How shall I know if I do choose the right?* asks the Prince of Morocco in Shakespeare's Merchant of Venice. There are three ways of deciding what to select. We can let ourselves be guided by our own experience of the language – experience gained by reading or from hearing the language naturally spoken. Secondly, we can rely for an answer on somebody who knows intuitively the right thing to say, though that person may not be able to explain why it is right. Thirdly, we can find a solution in a grammar book which is concerned not so much with facts as with subtle distinctions of thought, personal and inter-personal attitudes, and individual points of view. Notice I say 'not **so much** with facts'. There is always an element of fact in these problems – the exact words and phrases uttered (the linguistic facts) and the circumstances in which they were used (the non-linguistic facts). What turns these questions into problems is the element of choice and of subtle distinction which the student, learning English as foreign speech, may fail to appreciate or even to see.

It is this aspect of English grammar that the non-native speaker of the language finds most worrying. When to use or omit *the* or *a*; whether to say *I write* or *I'm writing, have written* or *wrote*; how to use *have been writing* and *had been writing*; what tenses to use with *if* or *since*; how to use *can, may, could, would, should, might, must*; whether to put the infinitive or the part of the verb ending in *-ing*; which preposition it is to be; whether to say *some* or *any, each* or *every*; where in a sentence to put adverbs; which of the four words *say, tell, explain, show* could fill the gap in *Please . . . me how this works*: these problems and others like them have been, and still are, very common in the learning of English as a foreign language.

Failure to master these distinctions may not always cause misunderstanding. You can often make your meaning clear without using *the* or *a* at all (see 3.2). Are they then superfluous, or have they roots that go deep into the thought of English speakers? To Henry Sweet *(New English Grammar, 1891)*, 'distinctions of verb-tense, and the use of prepositions and of verbal-groups (i.e. groups of words whose nucleus is an infinitive, participle or gerund)...are...highly developed in English, and are part of the genius of the language'. In the passage from which that quotation was drawn, Sweet was explaining how tense-forms and 'verbal-groups' in English take the place of the subjunctive in certain other languages. He went on to say, 'The faculty by which we instinctively know whether a certain form or construction is in accordance with the genius of the language or not is called "the linguistic sense". This faculty is naturally more highly developed in some people than in others; but it can always be strengthened by training, and the first business of grammar is to cultivate it as far as possible'.

Sweet had in mind readers for whom English was a mother-tongue. Now the problems of English grammar that bewilder the non-native speaker of English most, rarely seem to bother the native speaker at all. The latter may fumble over tense-forms and prepositions as children, and may be weak in command of the language in other respects. Yet unconsciously they get to know what satisfies the 'genius' of the language. Whether the native speaker's own usage is deliberate, precise and consistent, or automatic, haphazard and confused, what makes him or her decide to use *the, a,* or neither, or to choose one tense rather than another, may be as much as a mystery to native speakers – if they ever thought about it – as it is to the non-native learner. I assume that the readers of this book are among the many who are, or will be, obliged to think about it.

Students can ultimately acquire this 'faculty' through the constant reading of interesting, well-written English, or by being steeped for years in an English-speaking atmosphere. They stand a good chance of developing it if they are taught by men and women whose vision of the distinctions of thought involved is clear, and who can illustrate the distinctions effectively through vivid, memorable examples. It is very unlikely that they could acquire the faculty by being given abstract explanations first. Accurate statements about these problems are often particularly difficult to formulate, even for the trained linguist. They are far harder for students to understand if they have not already had the experience of the distinctions of thought in genuine examples within a proper context.

We can therefore imagine English grammar as a solid core of linguistic facts *(men, wrote, he wants to drive)* surrounded by a more nebulous area in which linguistic facts *(I wrote, I have written)* are often involved with subtle distinctions of thought, personal attitudes and points of view, as well as with non-linguistic facts, such as the particular circumstances in which certain words were uttered, thus:

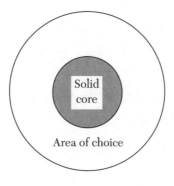

Fig. 1

A reasonable first aim in learning the grammar would be to master the solid core by learning the facts, whether one commits them to memory consciously or not. Mastering the rest of the grammar – which means learning to make the right choice – can only come from hearing, seeing, imitating and practising well-chosen examples in meaningful contexts – above all, from constantly reading the language, and attentively listening to it well-spoken. Abstract explanations will then help. But for explanations to help they must be accurate, strictly in accordance with genuine acceptable usage, and as clear as possible.

The following section summarises what I consider to be the contents of the 'solid core'. 'The rest', the area in which one has to learn to make the right choice, is the main subject of this book.

THE SOLID CORE

The basic rules of sentence structure, as exemplified in the patterns in Chapter 7; and the use of high-frequency verbs in the patterns appropriate to them. The patterns would include predicative adjectives and obligatory adverbials.

Rules for the pronunciation and spelling of regular noun plurals and of common irregular plurals.

Rules for the pronunciation, spelling and general use of the genitive with apostrophe.

Personal pronouns.

Basic uses of determiners, e.g. *some, any,* etc., as noun-modifiers and pronouns.

Use of not-too-complex nominal groups, consisting of pre-modifiers (including attributive adjectives), head-words, and commonly used post-modifier constructions; e.g. *that big black car in the road*.

Indefinite pronouns, e.g . *something*.

Use of the imperative; Simple Present of verbs; and Simple Past of regular verbs; and forms of *be, have* and *do*.

Rules for the pronunciation and spelling of the 3rd person singular, Present tense; and of the *-ing* and *-ed* forms of regular verbs.

Concord of subject and verb, where appropriate.

Use of the 'phrasal verb' constructions.

Irregular verbs.

Primary uses of modals.

Basic use of the Continuous with appropriate verbs.

Basic use of Present and Past Perfect.

The passive, with appropriate verb patterns.

Negation; *Yes/No* questions; and the various types of *Wh-* questions.

Basic uses of prepositions.

Adverbs, and adverb phrases, of manner, place, time and frequency.

Co-ordinations and apposition.

Compound and complex sentences, with co-ordinate and sub-ordinate clauses, finite and non-finite.

The above is an inventory of important items. It is not supposed to reflect an order in which those items should be taught or learnt.

(All these are fully discussed in *A Reference Grammar for Students of English*, R. A. Close, Longman 1985)

THE VALUE OF RULES

In the 'solid core' of fact, it is comparatively easy to formulate rules; though it is not quite so simple as we sometimes imagine. Many people, asked to state a rule for forming the plural of nouns in English, would say, 'Oh, just add-**s** to the singular.' But that is not all the story: it ignores certain aspects of the spelling, which can be covered if the rule is stated more fully, and ignores the important matter of pronunciation. Add the sound to the singular, *eye*, and you get *ice*. The plural of such a common noun as *nose* requires not only an-**s** but also an extra syllable. Nevertheless, about the 'solid core' the linguist can – by taking into account all the relevant facts – fairly easily draw up a series of statements which will serve as reliable rules for our own use of the language. Even these rules, however, may have to be learnt in instalments; and the important thing is not that they should be learnt in the abstract but that the learner should acquire the habit of applying them automatically in real acts of communication.

In the more difficult area of choice there are very few conclusions that the linguist can easily draw. 'Give me a simple rule for using the articles, or the tenses' is asking for the impossible. Usually, teachers deal with these problems of choice step by step through the application of over-simplified 'rules' that are easily teachable but are only a part of the truth. That is a sensible thing to do, especially with pupils who will never be able to learn more than the rudiments of English. Unfortunately, half-truths are not valid for very long. I am not suggesting that we should abandon them, but that we should realise their limitations. Examples of their inadequacy are given below.

INADEQUATE RULES AND OVER-SIMPLIFICATIONS

THE DEFINITE ARTICLE

'The definite article, *the*, is used to indicate an object of which there is only one example present.' This is demonstrated in the classroom by contrasting *a chair, a book, a picture* – one of many chairs etc. in the room – *with the door* – the single door – *the floor, the ceiling*. But confusion in the learner's mind begins when the teacher adds *the table*, the one and only table, forgetting that in a previous lesson that same article of furniture was used in ringing the changes on *This is a book*, thus: *This is a pen, This is a wall, This is a table.*

What is wrong? The definite article is used to indicate a solitary example. However, so is the indefinite article: it is quite correct to say *This is a table* when there is only one table to be seen. Furthermore, the definite article is used to indicate an object of which there are many examples present: in my mind's eye, I see a street full of houses and myself wearily walking from one to another, looking for the one to which I have been invited, and wondering, *which is the house?* Finally, the definite article is often not used with an object of which there is only one example. If Shakespeare were present at this discussion, there would be an object of which only one example has ever existed; yet we do not say *the Shakespeare* until we imagine that there is more than one example and we wish to distinguish, let us say, *the Shakespeare we study* from *the Shakespeare his mother knew.*

The Shakespeare we study is in fact a good example of how the definite article in English functions, as we shall see in Chapter 3. Proper nouns, such as *Shakespeare*, are not normally preceded by an article in English. The definite article in English helps to identify one example of a concept, or more than one, and to isolate the identified object or objects from another or from others. In English, we do not feel the need for such a device with a proper noun: we feel that the name itself is enough to identify the object we have in mind. It is only when we begin to form more than one image of the object bearing that name, and wish to distinguish one of those images from another, that we use the article as a signal that we are making such a distinction.

PRESENT CONTINUOUS

The Present Continuous as in *I'm writing*, is used for action performed at the time of speaking, the Simple Present, as in *I write*, for action performed habitually.' That is true in the examples *I am writing a book, Now you are reading it, I write a few hundred words every day* and in countless other cases. But the Simple Present is also used for action performed at the time of speaking. *I put my pen down at this point, get up and walk over to the window, thinking out what to say next*. I found myself saying those words quite naturally as I went through the motions.

In observing classes where English is being taught, and in reading manuscripts by prospective textbook writers, I am continually hearing and reading pronouncements such as the following: *We use the Present Continuous for what is happening now.* That is an example of an over-simplification which I would not call 'sensible'. It begs the question by using the Present Continuous as a way of trying to explain the use of the Present Continuous itself; and it overlooks the fact that we could equally well say: *We use the Simple Present for what happens now*, as in *I used to write all my letters. Now I type them.* Furthermore, though that pronouncement would be true of *Now we are going to the University*, if the statement were made while we were actually on our way there, it would not apply to an example like *John is already eighteen: he is going to the University now*, when that information was imparted at a moment when John was at home oversleeping after a late night. We have therefore, in this paragraph, had two different examples of the use of the Present Continuous; and we shall find others later. The first is perhaps the most natural one to start with. But what is important about it as an initial presentation of the Present Continuous is not the relation between that construction and the word *now*, or an adverbial of similar meaning, but the association between the Present Continuous and a physical motion which one can see or feel in progress while that construction is being used. We need to establish the association, for example, between the utterance *I'm drawing a map of Africa* (in answer to the question *What are you doing?*) while our fingers and our pencil are moving towards the production of the map; or to establish the association between, say, *She is skating beautifully*, spoken by a television commentator as we watch the skater moving to and fro across the television screen. In any case, with both the two different examples of the Continuous we have had in this paragraph, the essential feature is that an activity has already begun and has not yet ended when use of the Continuous is made.

Classroom English – the basis of much knowledge of English as a foreign language – is often artificial. It is unnatural when the teacher walks to the door, pulls the handle and announces, '*I'm opening the door*'. It would usually suit the words to the action on such an occasion more appropriately if the teacher said, '*I'm just going to open the door*' or '*I've just opened the door*'. In the same way, *I'm opening my book, Now I'm closing it, I'm switching on the light, I'm putting my pen on the desk*, as comments on what is happening now, would all be unnatural. Why? Because in such cases the teacher is commenting not on activity that has begun and is still in progress, but on a momentary act that could only be seen in a progressive state if performed very slowly or photographed by a slow-motion camera. If one wishes to demonstrate the Present Continuous while actually using that form, it would be more realistic to choose a verb referring to activity having duration, as in *Please be quiet for a minute or two, I'm writing an important letter;* or a verb referring to a series of momentary acts, as in *Hurry up or we'll be shut in. The caretaker is locking all the doors.*

When, in real life, does one have to comment on action at the time when it is being performed? Most of all, in these days, when commentating on radio or TV; when showing someone how to operate a machine, or how to prepare and cook food; perhaps when performing a conjuring trick; when making formal declarations; and so on. In a radio commentary on present action, the Simple Present and the Present Continuous may occur with equal frequency. The following from a television commentary on a track race is typical; *They're moving up to their marks. They're off! No that was a false start. The starter motions them back.* In an observation of the constructions occurring in such commentaries, it was noted that the Simple Present was used almost entirely in an account of a football match, the Present Continuous throughout a description of the Oxford and Cambridge boat-race. We cannot conclude from this either that the normal rules of English grammar do not apply to radio commentaries, or that one set of rules applies to football-commentator English, another to descriptions of university boat-races. The English of commentators may be more alive and more naturally 'correct' than the artificially systematised language of English teachers. The difference between the football match and the boat-race is interesting and will be explained later (see 5.2). As for other commentaries made at the time an action is performed, note:

(a) *Now watch me: I switch on the current and stand back.*

(b) *First, I make sure the gear is in neutral, and then I press the self starter.*

(c) *I pour the milk in slowly.*

(d) *Look carefully: I cut the string once, and I cut it again.*

(e) *I declare the meeting closed.*

That, too, is natural English. To dismiss it as professional jargon, or as a special case for which some label like Instantaneous or Demonstrative Present must be found, will not help to solve our problems. Nor will it help if we argue that what the commentator really means is *Every time I do this, I (habitually) switch/stand back/make sure,* etc. (S)he may mean that; but just as likely is the meaning: *This is what I do now.*

The Simple Present is certainly used to relate habitual action but that does not entitle us to say that the distinction between the act performed at the present moment and the act performed repeatedly in present time is shown in English by a difference in tense-form, except incidentally in certain common types of usage. That distinction is an important one in languages, and it is made in

English; but it is best shown in English by adverbial expressions or by the general context. The Simple Present is also used, as we have just seen, for an act performed now; and the Present Continuous can be used for habitual action: e.g. *You're always tapping on the table. Do stop it – It's a most annoying habit.* We must therefore look for other criteria in establishing the **essential** difference between these two tense-forms.

PRESENT PERFECT

'The Present Perfect, *I have written,* is used when we are specially concerned with the present results of past action, when the evidence of past action lies before us.' There is much truth in this. *Hurray, I've found it. Here it is,* and many similar examples would prove the 'rule'. Yet even here we have not found a factor (apart from the form of the construction) which is common to all examples of the Present Perfect. When I tell you that *I have lived in China,* I am not necessarily concerned with present results at all, I am not in China now and have not lived there for many years. Evidence may exist of my having lived there, but that evidence would be there just the same if I said *I lived in China before the War;* and I could still say *I have lived in China* though every shred of evidence had disappeared.

'The Present Perfect is used for recent happenings, the Simple Past, *I wrote,* for less recent.' That would be true in some examples, e.g. *It's stopped raining.* But the converse is also true: *The post came five minutes ago. England has had its civil wars* (the last was in the seventeenth century).

PRESENT PERFECT CONTINUOUS

'The Present Perfect Continuous, as in *I've been writing,* is used for action begun in the past and still going on in the present.' The exact opposite of the last part of this 'rule' ('still going on in the present') is so often true that I doubt the value of teaching it even as a temporary aid. The 'rule' applies to such examples as *I've been writing this book for six weeks* (and am still writing it) and *You've been learning English for six years* (and haven't stopped doing so). It does not apply to other examples, such as *Who's been sitting in my chair?* when whoever has been sitting in it has gone; or *'You've been working too hard',* said the doctor to the patient, motionless in bed.

PAST CONTINUOUS

'The Past Continuous, *I was writing,* is used for an action which is interrupted by another action in the past.' This is part of the traditional dogma of European language teachers. It sometimes applies to English, but only incidentally and by no means invariably. In *I was writing when the bell rang,* an interruption is implied. In *The bell was still ringing but I worked on without noticing it* or in *Someone was taking notes all the time you were speaking,* what is interrupted by what? *I was writing steadily throughout the afternoon* suggests that I was not interrupted for a moment.

PREPOSITIONS

'In referring to location, *in* is used with a capital city or town with a large number of inhabitants, *at* with a smaller place.' Insofar as this is true, it is a good example of the grammarian's prescription and of conventional usage. I have often found myself saying *in Edinburgh, in Prague, in Tokyo,* in conscious obedience to this 'rule', or to please such inhabitants of those great cities as might expect the rule to be observed for their benefit. Yet the 'rule' is not invariable. An aeroplane flying round the world can be said to stop *at Tokyo, at New Delhi, at Athens, at London,* on its way to New York; and we can say *in* the smallest of villages if that is the world we live in. But let us be careful not to make more rules out of these 'exceptions'. It is a fact (of which we can be certain) that we often use *at* with capital cities on air routes and *in* with villages when we are living in them; but a more fundamental point (of which admittedly we cannot be certain but which would make sense of both 'normal' and 'exceptional' usages) might be that we tend to associate *at* with what **we imagine** at the time of speaking to be a **point**, and *in* with what **we imagine** to be a **space**, as we shall see later.

Readers may come across other over-simplifications. They can always discover how far rules are inadequate by testing them against genuine and generally acceptable usage. Rules that break down under that test should not be regarded as axioms, but at best as temporary scaffolding poles which, if allowed to remain, could be mistaken for the real architecture of English and could prevent us from ever seeing it.

THE EFFECTS OF OVER-SIMPLIFICATION

Over-simplified 'rules' may seem to help, but they produce these effects:

(a) Usage is often distorted to support them. The teacher who places a pen firmly on the desk announcing, 'I am putting my pen on the desk', in obedience to the rule criticised earlier, is as guilty as the old-fashioned pedagogue who expected students to translate artificial sentences like *This is the pen of my aunt.*

(b) Hours are wasted not only on lessons teaching half-truths as if they were the whole truth, but also on doing exercises which require the student to choose between two constructions, both of which can be perfectly acceptable, though one of the two is falsely supposed to be 'wrong'. An instance of this is the exercise based on the 'rule' that *some* is used only with verbs in the affirmative, *any* only with the negative and interrogative. Expressions like *Would you like some more tea?* and *Any child could tell you that*, both perfectly good English, would be therefore considered 'incorrect'.

(c) Over-simplified rules will often remain firmly embedded in the learner's mind. A teacher I knew, whose mother-tongue had no exact equivalents of *a* and *the*, had once been instructed as follows:

'Use *a* when a noun is first introduced, and *the* when the same noun occurs again.' He believed that was the whole truth; and could never understand why the line from Shakespeare's Richard III, '*A horse, a horse, my kingdom for a horse*' should not be '*A horse, the horse, my kingdom for the horse.*'

(d) Above all, an inadequate basic rule will sooner or later have to be modified by a series of sub-rules and exceptions which may cause far more trouble in the end than a basic rule that is more accurate though less temptingly teachable.

COMMENTARY AND DISCUSSION POINTS

Close argues that many so-called classroom 'rules' are at best half truths. Can you give three examples?

He gives four clear problems which arise as a result of over-simplification. Which do you consider to be the most important?

Is there anything to be said for students forming their **own** rules on the basis of the examples they have met? The advantage is that the rules they formulate will reflect their experience of the language up to that point, and will certainly be in their own range of understanding. Could this be more useful than presenting students with rules which they may **not** understand?

2 Primary Distinctions

RULES AND EXCEPTIONS

The first thing I would ask of my readers is that they accept the weakness of any rule if educated usage does not support it. Though English speakers may sometimes be faced with a choice between one form and another, what they actually say and in what circumstances they say it are matters of fact, and a general statement about usage is incorrect if it is contradicted by the facts of generally accepted usage itself. It is not good enough to pretend that any usage is exceptional if it fails to fit the rules we believe.

We should therefore consider the difference between (a) irregularities in a system and (b) exceptions to a so-called rule. By the logic of Graeco-Latin grammar, which determined the thinking of teachers for centuries, every situation in language had its Rule and every Rule its Exceptions. Now we can establish a rule about some parts of the 'solid core' of English grammar, e.g. the plural of nouns, and we can note a number of irregularities in the system. We can call them 'exceptions to the rule' if we like: thus *cow, cows; goat, goats* but *sheep, sheep*. It is tempting to do this with the whole of the grammar and assume that there will be exceptions to any rule we formulate. This assumption is dangerous. Though we may say *cow, cows* but *sheep, sheep,* we cannot allow exceptions to the 'rule' that English-speakers make a mental distinction between one unit and more than one, whatever the name of that unit may be. If we believe that exceptions are inevitable, we can always make that an excuse when our 'rules' fail to work.

WORD ORDER

The fact that words are put together in patterns and in a certain order is very important in English grammar. For example, no alternative order is normally possible for the words in the following two sentences:

[1]   Harry has done that job very well.

[2]   That big black American car with the four men in it was stopped by the police.

However, it is not those particular words but what we call the 'elements' of sentence structure (e.g. subject, verb, object etc.) that must go in that order, thus:

[1]   Subject *(Harry)* + verb *(has done)* + object *(that job)* + adjunct, which is here an adverbial of manner *(very well)*.

[2] Determiner *(That)* + adjective referring to size *(big)* + adjective referring to colour *(black)* + adjective referring to origin *(American)* + head-word in a noun phrase *(car)* + prepositional phrase modifying the head-word *(with the four men in it)* + verb *(was stopped)* + prepositional phrase referring to the agent when the verb is passive *(by the police)*.

Now consider the following:

[3]   Please show me how this works.

[4]   The concert was | a success.
                                          | very good.
                                          | in the open air.
                                          | yesterday.

In example [3], only a limited set of verbs could replace *show* (e.g. *tell* could, but not *say*, or *explain*). In [4], what follows *was* is an obligatory element: the sentence would be incomplete without it; it can be either a noun *(success)*, adjective phrase *(very good)*, adverbial of place *(in the open air)* or adverbial of time *(yesterday)* and because of the tense of *was* it must be an adverbial of past time. Learning to construct sentences on such models is an essential process in mastering 'solid core' grammar, though the analysis is something that can be done at a later stage, if at all.

Words also go together in what we call collocations. For example, we try to *do good*, we *make a discovery*, we *pay attention* to somebody or something but *draw someone's attention* to it. We can only learn these collocations through use of the language or by finding suitable examples in a good modern dictionary.

ESSENTIAL AND INCIDENTAL FACTORS

In example [4] we could not replace *was* by *has been* because of a 'solid core' rule which tells us that we must have the Simple Past and not the Present Perfect, in association with an adverb of past time. But while this association between the Simple Past and a past time adverbial is an important factor, it is not **decisive** in our use of that tense. If I lose my watch and find it again a few days later, I can quite correctly say, *Oh, I found my watch,* without using any past time adverbial. Adverbials undoubtedly play a part in tense usage, but they are usually incidental factors, not essential ones. When I put on a raincoat, I usually take my umbrella too. When I wear an overcoat, I feel in my pocket for gloves. As a habit (and language is very much a matter of habit), I associate raincoat with umbrella, and overcoat with gloves. Thus I often put on my raincoat and pick up my umbrella automatically. But is it not possible that I perform **both** actions **primarily because I know it is raining?** Similarly, I may use the Simple Past, e.g. *I found*, in automatic association with an adverb like *yesterday* or *a moment ago*; but is it not possible that I use both expressions **primarily because my attention is focused, in both instances, on a specific point in past time detached from the present?**

We can also say *I've found my watch. Here it is*; and we can argue that the fact that I now have my watch and can show it to you is my reason for using the Present Perfect. But this present evidence – though, again, it is a very important factor – is still only an incidental one, since *I found my watch. Here it is* is equally acceptable.

Thus we can say:

> [5] I've found my watch. Here it is.
>
> [6] I found my watch. Here it is.
>
> [7] I found my watch yesterday.

But not [8] *I've found my watch yesterday.

Present evidence is only an **incidental** factor in the use of the Present Perfect in [5], since [6] is acceptable also; and because [6] is acceptable, the co-occurrence of *yesterday* is not the **essential** justification for the Simple Past in [7]. We must therefore look elsewhere (Chapter 5) for the **essential deciding factors** in our choice of the Simple Past and of the Present Perfect.

Nevertheless, it is a good idea in teaching the Simple Past to associate it at first with an adverbial of past time, especially a phrase ending in *ago*, which means 'back from now'. Later, it can be made clear that such an association, though always **possible**, is not **indispensable**. It may also be a good idea to introduce the contrast between the Simple Present and the Present Continuous with the help of adverbials, thus:

> [9]   We're speaking English now.
>
> [10] We always speak our own language at home.

But it would be wrong to leave pupils with a firm impression that the continuous is used **because** of association with now, while the Simple Present is used **because** of **always**. It would be just as correct to say

> [11] You're always writing. Don't you ever read a book?
>
> [12] I used to write my letters by hand. Now I type them.

Indeed, *always*, or a synonym for it, is necessary in [11] if the meaning is 'You never stop writing.' By firmly linking *now* with the continuous and *always* with the Simple Present, we may be **preventing our pupils from ever seeing the real distinction in meaning between the two forms**.

DISTINCTIONS OF THOUGHT

Since we are concerned in these problems with distinctions of thought, we should look for the **essential** factors both in the distinctions which all human beings find it necessary to make, and in those that are characteristic of the English-speaking people. Universal distinctions, e.g. between male and female, between one and more than one, will be obvious to the student. (Nonetheless, students may confuse *he* and *she* for purely phonological reasons; and may make errors in concord, e.g. putting a singular subject with plural verb, through careless application of the 'solid core' rules.) Other distinctions common to many languages, e.g. between completed and uncompleted activity, or between the act performed once and the frequent repetition of it, will be found in English, but indicated in a particular way which the student may not appreciate. Still other distinctions may be quite unfamiliar and students may not at first see that these distinctions are important or even that they are possible.

A language cannot help reflecting the ways of behaviour and thought of the people who speak it as their mother-tongue. English has developed through the centuries in the daily life of people whose instincts – or whose climate, or whatever it may be – impel them to physical action. They think in physical, rather than in abstract, logical or mystical terms. They are matter-of-fact. They like to get on with the job, to get things done, to get results. English-speakers reading this paragraph will want to know where it is all leading to. They are concerned with action, movement, direction, mathematically definite relationships in space. To them, there is an important difference between activity and achievement; still more between the word and the deed. They distinguish sharply between the idea and the reality, the general and the particular, the limitless and the strictly confined, the unspecified and the specific, the symbol and the thing it represents. To questions of fact, they want a straight answer; yes or no. They say, 'You know the answer, you remember it, forget it, like it – or you don't.' On the other hand, they are prepared to concede that the answer may depend entirely on one's point of view, on what exactly one has in mind, on where one wants to put the emphasis. Highly individualistic in a close-knit community, they distinguish between the person and people as a whole, between each one and everybody, between the unit and the mass.

That is the sort of attitude I see reflected in English grammar and the sort of criterion I shall be using in this book. One of the basic characteristics of that attitude is faith in the unalterable nature of fact. My first word of advice to those who want to understand English grammar is therefore: prefer the facts of authentic and acceptable usage to the grammarian's rules. The grammarian can provide students with rules which will prepare them for some of the facts they will meet, but not for all of them. There is no way of anticipating idiomatic conventions such as *go to school* side by side with *go to the theatre*, or *fail to do something* with *succeed in doing it*. However, I hope that by the time readers have finished this book they will be able to recognise and form for themselves the distinctions which have become stereotyped in such idiomatic phrases and which in the living language are constantly at work.

GRAMMAR AS A SYSTEM OF PAIRS: MARKED AND UNMARKED MEMBERS

We generally have to choose one or the other of a pair. One member of a pair may stand in contrast to the other; or each may stand in contrast, in its own way, to some element outside the pair. (R. W. Zandvoort, *Handbook of English Grammar* Longman, 1975 . . . we have in English the formal opposition illustrated by such pairs as *boy-boys*, and *boy-boy's*; among the personal pronouns we have the pair *I-we*, and *I-me*, and the set of three *he-she-it*. It is around such oppositions that the grammatical system of the language is to a large extent built up.') As we shall be continually referring in this book to contrast, let us use the symbol *v* instead of 'in contrast to'. Thus we may have *every v each; all v every; all v each; a v the; no article v a; no article v the*; and many others.

One member of a pair can be marked in some way; the other unmarked in that way; or both may be marked, each standing in contrast in a different way with something unmarked. To appreciate the principle involved here, notice the marked and unmarked members in the following pairs of words:

Unmarked		Marked
horse	v	mare
duck	v	drake
school	v	kindergarten

Ordinarily we speak of a *horse* whether the animal is male or female. In saying *mare* we are specially concerned with the fact that the animal is a female of the species. In other words, we use the marked form when we wish to make a particular distinction, the unmarked form when that distinction is not felt to be necessary. Notice that we can say *horse* even though we know the animal is female: in that case, we do not feel the distinction worth making, or it is not there that we wish to place the emphasis. Notice, also, that we **must** say *horse* when we wish to indicate that the creature is male, not female. (*Horse v stallion* forms a less common pair. In *stallion v mare* both members are marked in contrast to *horse*.) We can summarise the matter thus:

Unmarked	Marked
1 horse (sex of no concern; either sex)	mare (female in contrast to male)
2 horse (male in contrast to female)	

I shall call the first *horse* the **weak** unmarked form; the second *horse*, **strong**. With *duck* and *drake* the roles are reversed: the female happens to be unmarked, the male is the marked member. With *school* and *kindergarten* we have:

1 school (for children of all ages)	kindergarten (for small children only, not older)
2 school (for older children, above kindergarten age)	

The difference between the marked and the unmarked member of a pair is the particular distinction made on the marked member but not on the unmarked; for example, it is the distinction we wish to make when we use *mare* instead of *horse*, *drake* instead of *duck*, *kindergarten* instead of *school*. If you like, we might say that *horse*, *duck* and *school* are the norms, the other words are variants. What particular distinction do we wish to make when we use *mare* instead of *horse*, *drake* instead of *duck*? Is it a question of size? It might be, incidentally. Is it a question of colour? Again, it might be. But it is of course **primarily** one of sex. A distinctive feature of a kindergarten might be the smallness of the classroom furniture; but it is **primarily** the fact that it is designed for children of a certain age.

The contrast between unmarked and marked applies to both lexis (i.e. the words we use, *horse* or *mare*) and to grammar. I would regard the Simple Present as unmarked and the Present Continuous as marked: that is to say, the former is the norm, while the latter is used when we wish to **make some special emphasis**. As with *horse v mare*, *duck v drake*, *school v kindergarten*, there may be **incidental** differences between members of a grammatical pair, and **essential** ones. For example, the fact that *in* is used with reference to a capital city while *at* is used with a place with fewer inhabitants is not the essential distinction in the contrast *in v at*. You will not find CAPITAL CITY *v* VILLAGE among the primary distinctions which we now list.

PRIMARY DISTINCTIONS

We turn now to some of the most important distinctions of thought which are reflected in English grammatical structures. The various primary distinctions, and combinations of them will recur frequently in different contexts in later chapters.

A. Aspects of things that we refer to by nouns

1 CONCRETE *v* ABSTRACT

The distinction between a common noun, e.g. *table*, referring to something having physical substance, and an abstract noun, e.g. *kindness*, is still often taught in the earliest lessons in English grammar. However, far more important is the difference between unit nouns and mass nouns (see 5 below). What students have to learn about abstract nouns is really as follows:

(a) How they are formed, so that they can easily change: *Thank you for being kind* to *Thank you for your kindness*.

(b) With what other words they collocate. Thus: *We discovered something interesting* can be re-phrased *We made an interesting discovery*.

There is a distinction between concrete and abstract which appears in the following examples:

[13] We arrived at the right station.

[14] We arrived at the right conclusion.

The passive of [14] is quite acceptable, *The right conclusion was arrived at*, but is unlikely to occur with [13].

2 INANIMATE *v* ANIMATE

The distinction between animate (i.e. living) things and inanimate is especially important in deciding what words can act as subject or as object of what verbs. Note what kind of nouns can act as subject and object of *delight, enjoy, remember, remind*:

[15] Hector and his songs delighted the audience.

[16] The whole audience thoroughly enjoyed his performance.

[17] The ladies will always remember him and his music.

[18] Hector and his songs of long ago reminded the old folk of happier days.

Furthermore, the genitive with apostrophe *s* will not normally occur with a noun referring to something inanimate, though it does occur with nouns referring to human beings, human institutions, animals and birds; and the indirect object (see examples in Chapter 7) will always be a noun or pronoun referring to something animate, except in cases like *Please give my car a wash*.

We can take our passports to an officer or to an office, but only the 'animate' noun is allowable in the sentence *Take the officer your passport.*

3   HUMAN (AND NEAR-HUMAN) *v* NON-HUMAN

Within the inanimate v animate distinction, there is the question of whether or not something animate is human, or closely associated with human beings, or is completely impersonal. Notice how this affects the use of the interrogative *Who?*, which asks for the identity of a human being (though it could, in families that are very fond of pets, apply to a domestic animal); and of the interrogative *What?*, asking for the identity of something impersonal. It affects relative pronouns, *who* (or *that*) and *whom* being reserved for personal antecedents, and *which* (or *that*) for impersonal ones. *He* and *she* replace only nouns referring to male and female humans or to domestic animals whose sex is known and relevant. *She* is often used by a proud owner, usually male, when referring to a machine or ship *(She's a beauty, isn't she?),* though this odd usage should not be regarded as obligatory: *it* would be a perfectly acceptable alternative. Examples of human/near-human/non-human distinctions are:

[19] Who were those two men who arrived very late last night?

[20] What is that animal with black stripes? It looks like a horse, or a donkey, with pyjamas on.

[21] Has Bob taken the dog for a walk?
– Yes, he took it/him/her) out an hour ago.

4   SUBSTANCE *v* OBJECT CONSISTING OF THAT SUBSTANCE

We can have the substance *stone (A stone wall is a wall made of stone.),* or an object consisting of that substance *(Wait for me. I've a stone in my shoe.).* We can also have the substances *wood* and *metal*, and separate objects, e.g. *chairs*, made of those substances. There is a similar distinction between material (i.e. something that has been made, like *cloth* or *paper*) and a particular object, e.g. *a cloth, a paper*, composed of that material.

5   MASS *v* UNIT

We can regard the substance, *stone*, or the material, *cloth*, as an undivided mass, and the objects *stones, chairs, cloths* and *papers* as units that can be counted. This distinction is very important in modern English grammar, as we shall see (Chapter 3). Abstract nouns, e.g. *kindness, education,* tend to be mass nouns; but many can also occur as unit nouns *(You've done me a great kindness. He had a good education.)*; and some abstract nouns *(e.g. an idea, a scheme)* occur **only** as unit nouns. With the distinction between mass and unit, goes that between *amount* (of a mass) and *number* (of units).

6 CLASS (of substance or object) *v* **MEMBER** or example of that class

A cat, in *A cat is a domestic animal*, refers to the **whole class** of things which we could identify as cats; whereas *a cat*, in *Monty has a cat*, refers to **one member only** of that class. Similarly, *wood* in *Wood floats in water*, refers to the **whole class** of a certain substance; whereas *wood*, in a *piece of wood*, refers to **one example** of it only.

7 GENERAL *v* PARTICULAR

Language and *students* are general in the contexts *Language is a means of communication* and *Students often don't eat enough*. *The language* and *The students* are particular in *He speaks the language well* and *The students are drinking coffee*. But see 8.

8 UNSPECIFIED *v* SPECIFIED

In the last two examples of 7, *The language* and *The students* refer to a particular language and to particular students, but they are not, by themselves, specified. They would be specified in *The language we are now studying* and *The students who ought to be sitting here*.

9 UNLIMITED *v* LIMITED

We can have an unlimited amount or number, as in *Take any of this material, or any of these books that you want*, or a limited amount or number, as in *I hope you will leave some of it, or some of them, for me*. Unlimited choice is implied by *What book would you like?*, while *Which book?* limits the choice to a specified number. → *choose from a range of books.* | → *you have to choose among those more specific*

10 WHOLE *v* PART

We can have *all*, i.e. *the whole* of an amount or of a number, or *some*, i.e. part of that amount or number.

11 ONE *v* MORE THAN ONE

This is the well-known difference between singular and plural.

12 TWO *v* MORE THAN TWO

Both, each, either, neither, refer to two units; *all, each, every, any, none* refer to more than two.

B. Aspects of activity that we refer to by verbs

13 GENERAL *v* PARTICULAR (see 7 above)

We refer to the general activity of swimming in *Fish swim in water* but to particular performances of it in *We swim in the river every morning*. The continuous form of the verb is very unlikely to be used when the speaker is referring to the activity in general: it is much more likely to be used with reference to particular performances as in *I know where Dick and Harry are. They're swimming in the lake.*

14 The ACT as a WHOLE *v* the UNCOMPLETED ACTION (see 10 above)

The act as a whole is emphasised in *I've read your book;* the uncompleted action in *I've been reading it.*

15 The ACTION ITSELF *v* the ACTION FINISHED

Focus is on the action itself in *Drink,* as in *Drink a pint of milk a day;* in the action finished in *drink up,* in *You haven't finished your medicine – drink it up.*

16 The ACTION *v* the RESULT ACHIEVED

Focus is on the action in *do,* e.g. *What are you doing? Are you busy?* It is on the result in *make,* as in *I'm making some bookshelves.*
= the result.

17 An EVENT *v* a STATE OF AFFAIRS

The verb refers to an event occurring at a point in time, in *We moved to London in 1988,* but to a state of affairs lasting throughout a period of time in *We have lived here for eight years.* Notice how this affects the tense associated with *since:*

> [22] Since we moved here (since that event), we've made many new friends.

> [23] Since we've lived here (while that state of affairs has continued), many of our old friends have come to see us.

18 POINT-OF-TIME ACTION *v* ACTIVITY HAVING DURATION

In *I've shut the door, shut* refers to point-of-time action: while *He's shutting* refers to a series of acts, or to activity having duration, in:

> [24] It's time to go. The caretaker is shutting all the doors.

The continuous form of the verb is unlikely to occur in natural English with reference to a single point-of-time act: it is much more likely with activity having duration.

19 DYNAMIC *v* NON-DYNAMIC (or STATIVE)

Most verbs refer to 'dynamic activity' over which we have control and which can therefore be performed deliberately and purposefully: e.g. *look, listen, walk, run.* But certain verbs, called 'stative', do not refer to purposeful activity: they express a relationship, as in the case of *be* and *have,* or sensory or mental states, as in the case of *see, hear, know, understand*. 'Dynamic' verbs can easily occur in the continuous, with adverbs of manner (e.g. *carefully*) and with expressions of purpose; whereas 'stative' verbs will normally not occur under those conditions. Thus:

[25] I was looking at the signature carefully (adverb of manner) to make sure it was mine. (purpose)

but not *I was seeing it carefully to make sure etc.

20 MOVEMENT FROM ONE PLACE TO ANOTHER *v* NO SUCH MOVEMENT

Go, come, drive, fly all imply movement from place to place and are used with prepositions of movement *(to, into* etc see Chapter 9). *Be, stay, live, work* do not imply such movement and occur with prepositions of position *(at, in,* etc).

21 FREEDOM TO ACT *v* LACK OF FREEDOM

The modals, *will, shall, would, should, can, could, may, might, must* and *ought* will be considered (in Chapter 6) as expressing varying degrees of freedom to act, from absolute freedom to complete lack of it. They will also be considered as expressing various degrees of certainty on the part of the speaker with regard to the statement the speaker is making.

C. Aspects of time

22 UNLIMITED *v* LIMITED (see 9) (Page 66)

Unlimited time is expressed by the Present Tense only; limited time by Present, Past or Future.

23 PRESENT TIME *v* TIME NO LONGER, or NOT YET PRESENT

All time is considered as present until we give some indication (e.g. *yesterday, tomorrow*) that we have marked off part of it as non-present.

24 POINT-OF-TIME *v* PERIOD (see 17)

In *I had been waiting since the accident happened, that is to say for half an hour. I waited till the ambulance arrived*, the accident happened at one point of time, the ambulance arrived at another; *since* marks the point at which a period of time began; *till* marks the point at which a period ended; *for* signals the length of a period.

25 PERMANENT *v* TEMPORARY

Adjectives that can be used attributively (e.g. *a strong, healthy man*) tend to refer to a permanent condition, while those that occur only predicatively *(The baby is awake)* tend to refer to a temporary state of affairs.

NO D. Aspects of space

26 NO, or UNSPECIFIED DIMENSION *v* ONE, TWO or THREE DIMENSIONS

Unspecified dimension, or no dimension, is associated with *at*, e.g. *Wait at the door. Stop at that point;* whereas *on* is more often associated with one dimension (*on the line*) or two (*on the surface*), and *in* with three (*in a space or area*).

27 MOVEMENT *v* POSITION (see 20)

We can consider movement **to** a destination, position **at** that point, movement **away from** it, and position **away from** it, thus:

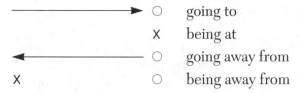

○	going to
X	being at
○	going away from
○	being away from

NO E. Degree

28 GRADABLE *v* UNGRADABLE

There can be degrees of hardness, softness, goodness, etc., so that we can say *very hard, (not) hard enough, too hard, harder, hardest,* and so on. But there are no degrees of, say, uniqueness, so that **very unique, *more unique,* etc. are unacceptable. *Hard* is therefore called gradable, *unique* ungradable.

A similar distinction can be applied to adverbs – *very carefully, (not) carefully enough* (gradable) but not **very completely* (ungradable). It can also be applied to verbs; *like* and *appreciate* are gradable, but *see* and *meet* are not; hence the different adverbial in I *like,* or *appreciate, that very much,* but I *see,* or *meet, him very often.*

F. Affirmative, negative, interrogative

29 AFFIRMATIVE ASSERTION *v* NEGATION or DOUBT

Some, already and *too* are normally associated with affirmative statements and with questions that expect or imply an affirmative answer. *Any, yet* and *either* are normally associated with negatives or with questions that seem prepared for either a negative or affirmative reply. Thus:

[26] I've found some mistakes in this book already.
- I've found some, too. Have you found some (or any)?
- I haven't found any yet.
- I haven't found any either.

G. Apposition and relative clauses

30 RESTRICTIVE *v* NON-RESTRICTIVE

Consider the following examples:

[27] Everything comes to the man who waits.

[28] Nothing could annoy my Uncle Tom, who was the most patient man alive.

[29] I know your friend Tom Jackson very well.

In [27], the relative clause, *who waits*, is restrictive or defining: it answers the question *What man?* In [28], the relative clause, *who was* etc., is non-restrictive; it does not answer the question *Which Uncle Tom?*, but supplies **additional** information about him. Similarly, in [29], *Tom Jackson* is in restrictive apposition to *your friend*: it tells us which of your friends. The significance of this is as follows: *that* could replace *who* in [27], but not in [28]; and commas, with a break in intonation, are obligatory in [28] but would not occur in [27] and [29].

H. Matters of fact

31 FACT *v* NON-FACT

Were refers to fact in *You were here yesterday,* but to non-fact in *I wish you were here today (but you're not).* Other factors affect linguistic choice and we must also take into account:

(a) What exactly **the speaker has in mind at the time of speaking**. The important thing is not what the object to which (s)he refers is in reality, but what the speaker imagines it to be at the time. '*At a place*' is 'right' if the speaker imagines that place as a point on the map. '*In it*', is 'right' if the speaker sees it as a space-area. We can say *the committee thinks* if we have in mind a body of people, or *the committee think* if we have in mind a body made up of **individual persons**. Both are acceptable, so long as the speaker does not change point of view erratically. The speaker may say *The committee have finished their work,* but not put *has* with *their,* or *have* with *its.* Nevertheless, in unscripted speech even educated and effective speakers change their mental image in the middle of a sentence; and thus produce 'mixed' forms. It is safer to avoid this in writing, which, as a more reflective process, affords the chance to ensure consistency.

(b) The speaker's point of view; and particularly the point in space or in time which is of primary concern to the speaker at the moment of speaking. The importance of the speaker's point of view is obvious in *here and there, this and that*. It will be found to play a considerable part in tense usage. It affects the use of *come* and *go, bring* and *take, up* and *down*. *Come* indicates movement in the same direction as the speaker, or towards the speaker's 'point of view' or 'point of primary concern', which might be either where (s)he is or where the person being addressed happens to be; *go*, in any other direction. *Bring (something)* corresponds more or less to *come with (it); take (it)*, more or less to *go with (it)*. *Up* indicates direction not only towards a higher physical level but also towards a place to which the speaker attaches greater importance, though within a certain area, e.g. a country; *down*, not only towards a lower level but also a place of lesser importance; although these considerations may be outweighed by others, such as *up north* and *down south*.

How the Right Choice is Made

The 'right choice' of construction might therefore be   ᵓ to result from an association between (a) the particular 'aspect' that the speaker has in mind and wishes to emphasise, and (b) the construction (s)he selects. That association must be acceptable to educated native speakers of the language. It may have to be adjusted according to the way in which individual words happen to be treated. For example, *an iron* is a household implement, originally made of the substance *iron*; but *a wood* usually signifies a group of trees. Moreover, the association must be the essential one. For instance, the distinction between permanent and temporary may help us to see why we can say *My aunt* is *unwell* but cannot say **My unwell aunt*. I might have that same distinction in mind when I say *My aunt is living in a furnished apartment, temporarily;* but that is not the **essential** distinction between *is living* and *lives*. We could not use the temporary/permanent contrast to justify *She's being unwell* (which might suggest that she is in the uncompleted act of being sea-sick).

Fixed Expressions and Freedom of Choice

There are a great many fixed expressions in which the speaker finds the right correlation readymade. In natural speech they are produced automatically. Take for example the expressions *to school* and *at school* in the contexts *In most countries all children now have to go to school* and *They stay at school until they are fourteen or fifteen*. In both cases we refer to the concept *school* in general, and use no article; we do not wish to specify the institution – in fact, our emphasis is on something else, namely the education given at school. In the first case we are interested in **movement**, *going (to)*; in the second, with **position**, **dimension unspecified**. Now, are *to the school, at the school, in school* or *in the school* 'correct'? Yes, all are if they correspond with what we mean; in other words, if we have good reason for using those marked forms, and if they reflect, in a linguistically conventional way, some special distinction that we wish to make. *To the school* (movement) and *at the school* (position) might be described as marked members of the pairs *to school* v *to the school* and *at school* v *at the school*, where we use the signal *the* to show that we are referring not to school in the abstract but to **one identifiable school** as distinct from another or from others or as distinct from something else. Thus:

> [30] In some countries parents are obliged to send their children to the school nearest their home.

> [31] I know Dr Berry – she taught at the school I used to go to.

Then we have the pair *at school* v *in school* in which we use the marked member, *in school*, to stress the idea of being in a space without specifying the institution:

> [32] You must stay in school till the bus comes to fetch you – it's far too wet to go out.

An example of *in the school* would be

> [33] Every room in the school is overcrowded. (a Head complaining about a single school)

Word-groups like *at school* and *in school* tend to form part of larger groups and to become associated with certain situations. Thus *stay at school* is customarily used to mean *stay at this place called school* or *continue to be a school pupil*, while *stay in school* is used to mean *remain inside the building*. A perfect command of English may therefore depend on the speaker's knowing what words and word-groups are commonly used in combination with one another and precisely in what social situation each is employed. But if that were invariably true the learner's task would be endless and English would not be free – as it is, to a remarkable extent – to adapt itself to new situations. The main argument of this book is that the kind of primary distinctions described in this chapter and discernible in stereotyped expressions like *stay at school* and *stay in school* are those that determine free and original usage.

COMMENTARY AND DISCUSSION POINTS

In this chapter Close stresses the difference between essential and incidental factors in particular grammatical usages. How can teachers avoid making partial rules which concentrate on incidental factors?

Can you list the **essential** factors which lie behind points:

Some v any

At v in

Use of *a* versus no article.

Examples of the present continuous relating to future time.

These will be discussed later in the book, but it may be helpful for the reader to try to identify the essential factors **before** reading on.

Close lists 31 Primary Distinctions, all of which are rather abstract. Do you think there is any point in introducing these distinctions in class? If not, how do you avoid the fact that any explanation you give must be a simplification, and can easily be an **over**-simplification?

Choose, for example, five of his Primary Distinctions such as:

Mass v unit

General v particular

Unlimited v limited

Permanent v temporary

Gradeable v ungradable

and find language examples which show the contrasts.

If you are not used to thinking of grammar in these very abstract terms, it is useful to go through all the Primary Distinctions until you are sure you understand them. It is combinations of these distinctions which determine grammatical usage and without a terminology of this kind it is difficult to discuss grammar clearly.

3 The Articles

3.1 INTRODUCTION

All English sentences have two main components – the Noun Phrase, of which a noun is the nucleus, and the Verb Phrase. The articles – *a*, *the* or zero (the concept of zero, which here refers to the absence of an article, is a very old one in the study of grammar, and is commonly used by modern grammarians) – are an important part of the noun phrase. They belong to a class of word now called 'determiners'. A determiner very often accompanies and precedes a common noun for this reason: a common noun is the name of a class of thing and with such a noun we usually have to indicate which member or members of the class, or what quantity of it, we have in mind. Determiners therefore either identify and are identifiers (answering the question *Which?*), or quantify and are quantifiers (answering the question *How much?* or *How many?*). The articles identify, definitely or indefinitely.

The problems with the articles are to decide whether to use:

zero or *a*
zero or *the*
a or *the*
singular or plural

The primary distinctions that apply to those four problems are:

mass *v* unit
general *v* particular
unspecified *v* specific
substance *v* object consisting of such substance
one *v* more than one.

The distinction between mass and unit is of prime importance in the use of the articles. There are nouns that are almost invariably mass nouns, e.g., *music*, *poetry*; others that are invariably unit nouns, e.g. *loaf, book, poem*; others that can be used either as mass nouns or as unit nouns. Those used as mass nouns are not preceded by *a*, nor used in the plural. Those used as unit nouns can have *a* and a plural. Generally speaking, mass nouns include the nouns of solid substances and materials *(stone, wood, cloth, paper)*; of liquids and gases *(water, smoke)* and of languages. Most abstract nouns are normally mass nouns, e.g. *advice, beauty*. Certain words, whose equivalent in other languages would occur in the plural, are singular mass nouns in English, e.g. *furniture, luggage, news*. Unit nouns include the names of persons, animals, plants *(man, horse, rose*); objects having a distinct shape *(ball, hammer)*; units of measurement *(hour, kilometre)*; and a few abstractions *(idea, nuisance)*.

The terms 'countable' (or 'count') and 'uncountable' are often used instead of mass and unit. I have avoided them in this book, having found that they often lead to confused thinking. Consider the statement '*Egg* is countable.' The things we call eggs are of course countable. *Egg*, the substance, is uncountable, as in the following dialogue:

Grandmother	I know what you had for breakfast this morning.
Grandchild	What did I have then?
Grandmother	Egg.
Grandchild	How you know?
Grandmother	Because you have egg on your chin.
Grandchild	Well, you're wrong. I had egg yesterday.

On the other hand, *money* is called an uncountable, although the counting of money must be one of the commonest of human activities. (I am indebted to Dr D. P. L. Dry for the story of the student who justified *People was everywhere* on the grounds that the people were uncountable!)

3.2 THE NOUN UNMARKED WITHOUT ANY ARTICLE

A set of pictures designed for teaching reading to native English-speaking children contained one like this:

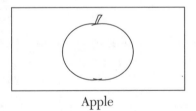

Apple

Fig. 2.

The children were expected to copy that picture, writing 'apple' at the bottom: not 'an apple' or 'the apple', but simply 'apple'. The designer of the picture had assumed that the need for the special distinction made by *a, an* or *the* had not yet arisen. The child's mind was not to be confused by the possibility of there being other apples, or other things from which the object the child was drawing had to be distinguished. The drawing filled the picture.

Take another example. According to an ancient story, before men began to build the Tower of Babel so that they could climb up to Heaven, they spoke one tongue. The idea of other languages had never occurred to them. In such a situation we would say, 'People used language to speak with one another,' just as we can still say, 'Human beings are superior to animals in that they use language to convey their thoughts.' Let us represent 'language' thus:

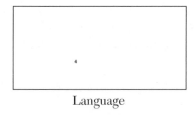

Language

Fig. 3

3.3 THE NOUN MARKED TO INDICATE AN UNSPECIFIED NUMBER OF UNITS

Later in the set of pictures mentioned above, this illustration was provided:

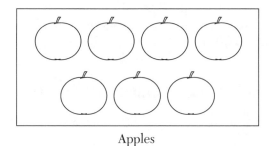

Apples

Fig. 4

The picture contained, as it happened, seven apples. But the actual number was not important. The purpose of the exercise was simply to present children with a picture filled with apples, to let them copy it and write 'apples' at the bottom.

The story of Babel goes on to tell us that as a punishment for their trying to climb up to Heaven humans were made to speak different languages. Figure 3 then becomes:

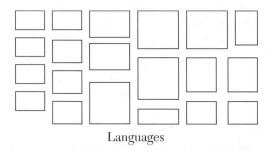

Languages

Fig. 5

A film or television camera could move away from Fig. 2 to produce Fig. 4 – telescopically as it were. It could take a close-up of Fig. 3 to produce Fig. 5 – microscopically. Note that if Fig. 3 represented a mass of water, the camera moving towards it would show a smaller area of water; away from it, a larger area; but it would not show water as a group of units.

In Fig. 2 and Fig. 3 we have an unmarked form; we are concerned with an undivided whole; the concept in general; an example of the concept not distinguished from other examples or from different concepts; the concept that fills the picture. In Fig. 4 and Fig. 5 we are using a marked form to show that we are particularly concerned with the two concepts in terms of units – with apples and languages in general. The choice of *apple* v *apples* or *language* v *languages* is therefore a matter of **concept in general v units in general**.

3.4 THE NOUN MARKED TO INDICATE ONE, UNSPECIFIED EXAMPLE

Select any one of the units in Fig. 4 or Fig. 5. You now have one complete example of the concept – an apple or a language – an example that is a separate, complete unit by itself. 'An apple' or 'a language' could be written under each one of the units in Fig. 4 and Fig 5. We could express *apple* v *an apple* as **concept in general v one complete, independent but unspecified example of it**.

An (before a vowel sound) and *a* (before a consonant sound) might be considered as unemphasised forms of *one*. In the pair *a* (or *an*) v *one*, we use the marked form *one* to stress the idea of 'one and not more than one', or 'one and not another', as in

  [1] There's only one apple left.

  or

  [2] One man's meat is another man's poison.

We also use *one* as a substitute for a noun, as in

  [3] Will you have an apple?
     – Thank you, I have one. (i.e. I have an apple).

Note also the use of *one*, not *a*, in a sentence like

  [4] One day, as we were sitting quietly in the garden, an elephant walked in.

Note that *an apple* is one of all the things called by that name, i.e. one of a class. In that formula, **one of a class**, the emphasis can fall on **class** or on the quantity, **one**. Notice how this difference of emphasis operates in the following table:

Singular	Plural	Emphasis on
This is an apple.	These are apples.	Class
I'd like an apple.	I'd like some apples.	Quantity + class

Note also that *a language* is an independent whole; it is not merely a fragment or sample. A fragment or sample of language would be *language* with the zero article, as in *This sentence contains language*. There, I am using *language* to mean, not *language* in general, but one sample of it, although the same form is used for both. Likewise, a fragment of apple is simply *apple*, just as a trace of egg is simply *egg*. If we are concerned with the size of the sample, we can use *some*, as in:

	Emphasis on
This is water.	Class
May I have some water?	Quantity + class

A is by tradition called 'the indefinite article'. It can in fact point to both a completely indefinite unit (*I want a pencil* – any one will do) or a more definite one (*A man called to see you while you were out. Here's his card*). In any case, we may call it an **indefinite identifier**.

3.5 The Plural of 'An Apple', 'A Language'

Next, pick out more than one of the units in Fig. 4 and Fig. 5, and you have *apples* and *languages*. This is the same form as for 3.3, and explains why the same word *languages* could be translated into French in two ways, namely *les langues* (languages in general), *des langues* (more than one language). To stress the quantity 'more than one', we can use one of the quantifiers that will be discussed in the next chapter, e.g. *some, a few, a lot of*. So the difference in emphasis mentioned in 3.4 is clearly made in the plural. There is emphasis on **quantity** in *some eggs* in

[5]   Is there anything else you want, madam?
       – Yes. I'd like some eggs please.

but emphasis on the **class of thing** in

[6]   Would you like eggs for breakfast, or something else?

3.6 The Noun Marked with 'The'

Select one of the units from Fig. 4 again. Which one have you chosen, *this* one or *that* one? Let us put a mark round the one you have chosen. We are now concerned with **one specified unit** and no other. Now we have *the apple*. Which apple? The one we have marked, as distinct from all the rest.

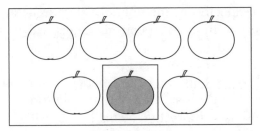

This is the Apple

Fig. 6

Once the unit has been identified, *the* serves as a weak form for *this* or *that* and makes it unnecessary for those words to be repeated. Note that *this* and *that*, and other definite identifiers such as *these, those, my, your, his, her, our, their* and a name with apostrophe *s*, e.g. *Shakespeare's*, are felt to be sufficient by themselves to identify the thing we are talking about. They are not accompanied by *the*, so that **the Shakespeare's theatre* is unacceptable. On the other hand, *the* is not sufficient by itself to identify the unit. It functions as a **signal of specification** – a signal by which the speaker conveys the message 'You know, or will know, the thing I mean.' The actual specification is provided by something else: see 3.15. In any case, if I say *Take the apple* I am assuming you know which one I mean. Notice also that while *this* and *that* can be used as pronouns, *the* cannot be. I can say *Take this (one)* or *that (one)* or *Take it*, but not **Take the*.

Now if all the units in Fig. 6 except the one marked were fruit other than apples, then in saying *Take the apple* I would be specifying that object called an apple as distinct from objects not belonging to that class. And if all the objects in Fig. 6 were taken away except the one marked, so that there was only one object in front of us, namely an apple, then in saying *Take the apple*, I would obviously be specifying that object.

The functions of *the* might be illustrated as follows:

← Very interesting!

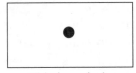

This is a circle.

  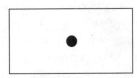

(a) The circle we have chosen is the third one.

(b) The circle – not the triangle or the square.

(c) The circle – you know which one I mean.

By using *the* we can specify one member of a class, as in (a); or specify one class of thing from others, as in (b); or specify an object which, in the context, is the only example of its kind.

This 'only example of its kind' can bear a mark of distinction in a double sense: it is distinguished from other things by its solitariness, and it can acquire distinction in the sense of 'prestige'. This is noticeable in *the President, the Headmaster, the Rector*.

The three categories are marked by differences of stress, noticeable when the noun is preceded by an adjective; thus:

(a) *Which will you have, the 'red apple or the 'green one?*   (Stress on the adjectives, *red* and *green*.)

(b) *The young 'student often thinks he knows more than the experienced 'teacher.*   (Stress on the nouns.)

(c) *The dis'tinguished 'president of our country. The 'blue 'sea.*   (Stress on both adjectives and nouns, more or less equally.)

Examples of the three categories are:

(a) [7]   Here are two apples: you may have the bigger one.

[8]   Here are three: we'll cut the biggest in half.

(b) [9]   Which is the heavier, the egg or this 'stone? The 'stone.

[10]   The lion (an imaginary representative of a class, as distinct from animals of other classes) is the king of beasts.

(c) [11]   The table – the one I am writing at.

[12]   The ceiling – the ceiling of this room.

[13]   The President (of our country) will arrive at half past two.

[14]   The sun (the sun we all know) sets in the west.

There is another way of looking at the (c) examples. If we consider the uses listed for *the*, we see that a certain point in the pattern is picked out from the rest; some object or point is specially marked. Imagine a square which contains a plan of your room or of your house, or a map of the district you live in; and that X represents a specified object in the room, or part of your house, or place in the town. In referring to that object or whatever it may be, you and the person you are addressing may know that other objects of the same class exist, but you both know perfectly well which one you have in mind. In English, we are constantly referring to definite, marked objects and places on the map of our domestic, social and personal experience. Thus, on the plan of my room I indicate *the door, the ceiling*; of my house, *the kitchen, the stairs*; of the ground where my house stands, *the garden, the lawn*; of the surroundings, *the road, the pavement*; of the district I live in, the *post office, the bank*; beyond, *the country, the sky*. I do not give these objects an exclusive name, such as *London*; I use a name that can be applied to other objects of the same kind.

Whichever way one looks at it, therefore, *a v the* is a question of **unspecified unit v unit specified in the context, or assumed by the speaker to be identifiable by the hearer**.

3.7 'THE' WITH THE PLURAL FORM OF THE NOUN

The apples, the languages, can then be explained as specific units, corresponding to *these* or *those apples*, etc. The pronoun in the plural would be *Take these, or those. Take the ones you have chosen. Take them*. There would be the same change of emphasis as with the singular examples in 3.6, but in the plural:

(a) [15]   These are not the apples I ordered.

(b) [16]   Divide the sheep from the goats.

(c) [17]   The stars are very bright tonight.

We do not, however, use the plural form to refer to specified fragments of a mass, so that *apples* or *languages* do not mean 'pieces of apples' or 'samples of language'. We would have to refer to specified fragments by such expressions as *pieces of apple, traces of egg, pieces of language* or *drops of water*. *Drops of water* will be discussed further in 3.15

3.8 SUMMARY OF THE USES OF THE ARTICLE

We can now make up a set of six 'aspects' for the uses of the articles in modern English, thus:

Aspect	Examples		Meaning
1	apple	language	the concept in general, the mass or sample of a mass; the unmarked form
2	apples	languages	the concept in general, but seen as a complete collection of units
3	an apple	a language	one, complete, unspecified unit chosen from the whole collection
4	apples	languages	more than one of those units – but not the whole lot

| 5 | the apple | the language | one example, either a complete unit or a sample, assumed by the speaker to be identifiable by the hearer |
| 6 | the apples | the languages | more than one identifiable unit (but not more than one identifiable sample) |

Potentially, every noun in English could be considered from each of those six points of view. In practice, because of the nature of the things we talk about, or because of the native English-speaker's conception of them, or for historical reasons, or simply because of fashion, some nouns fill all six of those positions more easily and frequently than others do. *Stone*, the substance from which buildings and statues are made, fills positions 1 and 5; *stone*, the object that one can pick up and throw, fills positions 2,3,4,5 and 6. *Man* can fill all six positions, even the first (*Man is a thinking animal*). The abstract mass noun, *knowledge*, besides filling positions 1 and 5, could fill 3 also (*A knowledge of English is essential*); but *knowledges* is a potential rather than an actual usage: it could occur in literature, but ordinary users of English would be wise to leave it to creative writers to experiment with.

For ordinary purposes, nouns fall into three groups according to the articles they require:

(i) **Proper nouns**, e.g. *Shakespeare*, which normally occur in aspect 1 only.

(ii) **Unit nouns**, e.g. *apple*, which normally occur in all six aspects except the first, thus:

2 Apples grow on trees.
3 This is an apple. Here is an apple.
4 These are apples. Here are some apples.
5 This is the apple mentioned in 3.
6 These are the apples mentioned in 4.

A few unit nouns would normally occur only in aspect 5, *e.g. the sun, the moon, the sea, the sky*, as already discussed.

(iii) **Mass nouns**, e.g. *water, music*, which normally occur only in aspects 1 and 5, e.g.

1 Water is heavier than air. This is water, not oil.

5 The water here is excellent.

The dividing line between those groups is not always easy to draw. Is *breakfast*, in *Breakfast is at eight*, a unit noun used as a mass noun? The difficulty of drawing a line, as well as the fact that there is a line to be drawn, emerges from the following test:

Apply the question *What is. . .?* to *apple, knowledge, sea* and we shall get *What is an apple? What is knowledge? What is the sea?* With other nouns we could produce either *What is iron?* or *What is an iron?, What is language?* or *What is a language?* With regard to *breakfast*, the normal native-English form of the question would be *What is breakfast?*

3.9 ARTICLES WITH PROPER NOUNS

We have already had *the Shakespeare*. We could also have *a Shakespeare*, i.e. a man with that kind of genius; and even *Shakespeares*, as in *There are not many Shakespeares in the world* (i.e. not many people like him). *The* is often used with family names, as in *the Barretts*, the family of people named Barrett.

Names of countries and other geographical areas begin with *the* when they are composed of unit nouns: *The United States, the British Isles, the Philippines*, are examples. Columbus, sailing west to reach India, reached several new Indias instead, and gave us *the West Indies.*

Apart from countries with political boundaries, such as those just quoted, certain geographical features which have to be distinguished one from another also have names beginning with *the. The Red Sea* is a specified sea, and so is *the Indian Ocean. The Giant Mountains* form a distinctive mountain range. *The River Nile* is that river and no other. The class-word can be omitted when the specifying word is sufficient to identify the feature: *The Mediterranean* (Sea), *the Pacific* (Ocean), *the Sahara* (Desert), *the* (River) *Ganges*. Note the effect of omitting' 'islands' and 'mountains': *the Philippine Islands, the Philippines; the Himalaya Mountains, the Himalayas.* The unit noun cannot be omitted when the modifying word by itself is inadequate identification: *the Red, the Indian, the Giants, the British* (as an abbreviation for *the British Isles*) could be applied to too many other things for the meaning to be clear.

The has long been a signal of specification for inns, taverns and hotels – *the Crown* (Inn), *the Elephant and Castle* (Tavern), *the Grand* (Hotel). Names of newspapers and periodicals are also preceded by the – *The Times, The Lancet, The Asahi, The Mainichi* – whether as an indication that one must be distinguished from another, or to indicate, for example, the one and only *Times.*

The Bible (literally 'the book') is a solitary member of its class, as is *the Koran*, or *the Odyssey*, or *the Iliad*. But we can borrow *a bible*, i.e. a copy of the Bible, just as we can borrow a 'Hamlet' or a 'War and Peace'.

One way of tracing the tendencies of living grammar is by observing native speakers in the act of creating their own idiom. I once worked in Crespel Street in Brussels for an organisation that was looking for other premises. We found what we wanted in Avenue Marnix, and referred to it as 'the Marnix building'. Soon, perhaps in imitation of those whose lead we followed socially, we were calling it 'the Marnix'. But our original office remained 'Crespel'. Thus, from Crespel, we would say, 'Are these things going over to the Marnix?'; but, speaking from the new building, 'My books are still over at Crespel.' (See 3.14)

It may be in such circumstances that English usage has grown up with apparent inconsistency in the use of the articles, as in other respects. With many of the names used in daily life by English-speakers, there is no way, without becoming intimately acquainted with that life, of telling when convention or fashion or accident will decide whether we say *the Marnix building* or *the Marnix* or just *Marnix*. All three are possible in English: one has to know which happens to have been adopted in each case. Students need not worry about the parochial whims of British or American speakers unless they wish to make a special study of them. But they do need to know in what ways the language can operate on such occasions. In the case of life in Britain, it operates with the following results:

(a) *Buckingham Palace, Hampton Court, St Paul's Cathedral, Victoria Station* (*or simply Victoria*), *London Bridge.*

(b) *The Tower of London* (or the *Tower*), *the Strand, the Edgware Road* (the road leading to Edgware), *the Old Vic* (Theatre), *the British Museum.*

One might rationalise some of these usages by arguing, for example, that with *London University* we are not admitting the need for specification – there is only one university in London and this is it (1962); whereas with *the London Library* we have in mind the existence of other libraries, in London and elsewhere, but this is the one we are specifying. Similarly, *Edinburgh University* and *the Edinburgh Festival.* However, when the unit word precedes the proper noun, *the* is used in any case: *The Tower of London, the University of London,* etc. *The* being a mark of distinction, *the University of Oxford* is felt to be more ceremonial than *Oxford University.*

3.10 Mass Nouns Used as Unit Nouns

Which abstractions and substances are customarily conceived as units in English is a matter of fact, and the student must observe the facts in use. A good modern dictionary will help here. The student will find that *Virtue is its own reward,* that *Patience is a virtue* and that *Faith, hope and charity are virtues;* that we speak of *faiths,* but to mean religions, and *charities* to mean not 'acts of charity' but charitable organisations. We speak of *doubts and injustices* i.e. matters in which we have doubt, and acts of injustice, but not *justices,* unless we are referring to judges. *Information* and *progress* would only occur in normal English in aspects 1 and 5(See 3.8) and so would *advice. News* though plural in form, takes a singular verb and also occurs only in aspects 1 and 5. *Weather* is usually found only in the same two aspects, though we find the expression *go out in all weathers*, where it can be used in aspect 2.

3.11 CLASSIFIERS USED WITH MASS NOUNS

One example of a substance or material is often indicated in English by 'classifiers', rather as in Chinese. The commonest and most useful classifier is *piece*, which can be used with abstractions as well as substances; e.g. a *piece of paper, of bread, of advice, of information, of news*. No shape is suggested by *piece*, but a piece of a more definite form can be indicated by *slice, strip, grain, stick, lump, heap, ball, sheet, block*, and similar words in constant household use. We can have *a slice of bread, cake or meat; a strip of cloth, of land; a grain of rice, of corn; a stick of chalk, of dynamite; a lump of lead, of coal; a heap of earth, of rubbish; a ball of wool; a sheet of paper, of metal rolled thin; a block of wood, of ice*. Colloquially, we can have *a bit* (i.e. a small piece) of anything. Some words have their own classifiers: *a loaf of bread, a joint of meat, a rasher of bacon, a clod of earth*. Similarly, we speak of *a blade of grass;* but we can pick out *a* (single) *hair* from the hair which grows on our heads. *Money* is a mass noun; the corresponding unit noun is *coin*, or *note*, or *pound, dollar* etc. All the classifiers mentioned above refer to solids, though we can speak metaphorically of *a sheet of water*, referring to its smooth surface. The liquid equivalent of *bit* would be *drop*.

When we do find a word for a substance or abstraction used with *a* it is either to indicate a kind of that substance or a finished product consisting of it. *A good wine* is a good **kind** of wine; *a bread* is a kind of bread, not *a loaf*. The same could be said of *an iron, a paper, a cloth*. But also and commonly *an iron* is a household implement; *a paper* is a newspaper, a written report or dissertation, or a set of examination questions; *a cloth* is the finished article spread over a table, or a small piece of cloth for cleaning. Similarly, *a work* is a product of work, a new creation. We speak of *a work of art, the works of Dickens, the devil and all his works*. Ordinary human beings merely *do a job*.

3.12 'PEOPLE' AND NATIONALITIES

With its individualistic concept of society, English envisages people only as separate units. If the question asked in 3.8 were applied to *people*, we would usually expect *What are people?* However, *people* can refer either to two or more persons considered together, or to a racial group. *The people* also means 'the general public'. Considered according to the six aspects in 3.8, *people* fits into the following scheme:

Aspect	Individual	Human beings	Racial group
1	person	—	—
2	persons	people	peoples (racial groups in general)
3	a person	—	a people (a racial group)
4	persons	people	peoples (more than one racial group)
5	the person		the people (the group, the public)
6	the persons	the people	the peoples (the racial groups)

People is followed by a plural verb, invariably when it means *persons,* and often when it refers to one racial group. *Persons,* instead of *people,* is typical of official English, e.g. *All persons who have not yet registered should do so without delay.*

Nationalities present a special problem, and we can only tell from experience or from a detailed reference book what names are appropriate to inhabitants, for example, of China, Egypt, Finland, Scotland, Switzerland, etc (see *A Grammar of Contemporary English,* by Quirk, Greenbaum, Leech and Svartvik, section 4.33). What we are concerned with here is the use of articles before such names. There are three main groups of nationality names:

(i) *A German*, plural *Germans;* similarly, *African, American, Russian,* etc.

(ii) *A Frenchman,* plural *Frenchmen;* similarly *Dutchman, Englishman, Irishman, Scotsman, Welshman.*

(iii) *A Chinese,* plural *Chinese;* similarly, *Japanese, Portuguese, Swiss.*

There is a further complication: we can say *one Frenchman,* two *Frenchmen,* etc. referring to individual members of a certain race; or *Frenchmen* or *the French* referring to that race in general.

[18a] The French drink wine.
[18b] The Frenchmen at that table over there are drinking vodka.

[19a] The Chinese like good food.
[19b] The Chinese sitting at that table are not eating anything.

[20a] The English like tea.
[20b] The Englishmen at that table over there are drinking sakú.

[21a] The Germans drink beer.
[21b] The Germans at the table are drinking mineral water.

The (a) examples have what is called 'generic' reference, whereas the (b) examples refer in each case to two or more individual members of the race named.

3.13 Unit Nouns Unmarked by 'A' or 'The'

Instances of unit-words in aspect 1 (see 3.8) are:

(a) **Notices**: *Footpath to beach* (notice seen at holiday resort).

(b) **Notes**: as in words *italicised* in *brackets* in *line* above.

(c) **Signs and labels**: *Arrow-head, fifth century* (in a museum), *Edgeware Road* (street sign).

(d) **Newspaper headlines**: *Bride-to-be Abducted at Church Gate.* Here, the absence of articles, besides saving space, tempts the reader to look for the specific details provided in the article below the headline.

(e) **Telegrams:** WIRE DATE CONTRACT SIGNED LETTER FOLLOWS. The receiver of this telegram should know which contract and which date were meant: in any case, the 'letter that follows' would supply the necessary specification.

(f) Certain **words in constant, communal use**, when specification is no longer felt by the community concerned to be necessary: *School begins next Monday. Term ends on December 19th.* British (and other) people commonly refer to their parliament as *Parliament* (no article); members of trades unions and other associations refer to their own annual conference as *Conference*.

(g) **Relationships used as proper nouns**: *Father says we mustn't. Give it to Mother. Thank you, Uncle. Baby, Nurse* and *Sister* (meaning 'senior nurse') can also be used in this way. Names of certain ranks and titles are used likewise: *Yes, Colonel. Carry on, Sergeant. I'm feeling much better, Doctor. That's all I know, Inspector* (of police); similarly, *Officer* and *Constable* in the police-force. This usage would not apply to persons of rank high above the level of the man in the street. One would therefore speak of *the King, the Duke, the President,* but not say **I'm happy to meet you, Duke.* One could always address an important man as *sir*, or a lady as *madam*.

(h) **Names of definite appointments.** Note: *He is a bank manager* – he is a member of that class. But he is *Manager of the Westminster Bank*. Similarly, *S(he) is President of the Republic, Rector of the University, Director of the Department*. In these last four examples, *the Manager, the President,* etc. are also possible and in fact add a tone of distinction to the title as previously mentioned. Observe the difference between *He was (the) Minister of Finance* (of that particular country, at that particular date), and *He was a Minister of Finance* (one of a series of Ministers of Finance).

(i) In certain types of expression where **words are put in couples** or in a list: *They became man and wife. People worked day and night, in office, field and factory.*

(j) With a **noun in apposition to another**: *Thomas Hardy*, author *of 'Tess of the d' Urbervilles'*. Omission of *the* in this case is not obligatory.

There are many fixed expressions composed of preposition + noun (e.g. *in fact*) or verb + noun (*give way*) in which we are not concerned with a specific example of the concept represented by the noun. Other examples: *in doubt, at ease, in general, at rest, in time, at war, at work; do harm, make peace, make progress*. The instances just quoted are of abstractions and it is understandable that they should occur with the zero article. But unit-words can also fit into this pattern when we are concerned not with a particular example of the concept but with, for example:

(a) an action communally associated with the object referred to: *go to bed, be in bed, get out of bed; go to church* (to pray, to attend a service); *go to hospital, be in hospital* (for treatment); *go to prison* (as a punishment); *go to school* (to study or teach); *go to university.*

(b) with the class of object, rather than any particular example of it, by which something is conveyed: *to go by bus, by car, by coach, on foot, by plane, by sea, by train; to send a letter by hand, by special messenger.* (Note the difference *by sea* and *by the sea* = beside the sea.)

(c) with the idea in general, or the thing in the abstract: *at dawn, on edge, in goal, in hand, at night, in person, in question, on record, in reply, at sea.*

Such word-groups tend to form when they express a fixed idea that constantly occurs in a community and when it is not felt necessary to specify the object represented by the noun. When one of those nouns is used to refer to a specific object or to express a different idea, then the fixed expression is no longer operative.

Specification is sometimes accompanied by a change of preposition, notably from *at* (unmarked, unspecified dimension) to *on* or *in*, where dimension is more clearly indicated (see Chapter 9) e.g. *at sea*, but *on the sea* (on the surface) and *in the sea* (in the water); *at night*, but *in* or *during, the night* (a specific night, or *the night* as distinct from *the day*).

It should be noted that the kind of expressions just dealt with must be accepted by the community; that in some situations they are optional (one can say *in spring, summer, autumn, winter* or *in the spring* etc., *go to university* or *go to the university*); while in some situations they have not found acceptance at all (e.g. we say *in bed* but not **on bed, *in chair,* or **on chair*). On the other hand, in some situations a different pattern has become established: e.g. *go to the theatre to see a play* or *to the station to catch a train; in the morning, in the afternoon, in the evening.* In these last examples we find the tendency noted earlier of marking off known points on the map, either in space (*the theatre/the cinema/the bank*) or in time (*the afternoon/the evening; the summer/the winter*).

3.14 MAN v THE ANIMALS

Why *man* but *the animals*? *Home is where one starts from* (T. S. Eliot, 'East Coker'). We say, '*This is home. We're at home. Go out, and come home again.*' There is no need to specify which home, or this part of the map as distinct from another. That kind of specification only begins when we venture away from our point of primary concern. But when the point of primary concern becomes the school, as it does with educationists, they can properly ask, '*Should moral education be given at school or in the home?*' (Note, too the change of preposition, as just discussed) *Crespel* was '*home*'; *the Marnix,* a definite sector of the outside world. Londoners live *in town,* but like to spend their holidays *in the country* or *by the sea.* In Japan, they go from *Tokyo* down to *the Kansai.* It is perhaps typical of the human mind, at least of the English-speaking mind, that each individual, should regard him or herself as such a centre, surveying the rest of creation, e. g. *children* (in general) or *the child* (imaginary representation of that class), *the animals* and *the birds* (the different classes of animals and birds) as categories of objects in the world outside them.

3.15 WHEN IS A NOUN 'SPECIFIED'?

When is a noun sufficiently specified for *a* before it to become *the*? In *David Jones is a doctor, a doctor* is considered unspecified. David is one of all the doctors in the world. *A doctor* is still unspecified if we add a descriptive adjective, e.g. *good.* All we are then saying is that David is a member of the whole class of good doctors.

There are three conditions in which *a* + noun can be replaced by *the* + noun:

(a) when reference is made **back** to something already said:

[22] A doctor and a policeman happened to be standing nearby when the accident happened. The doctor (i.e. the one just mentioned) was David Jones.

(b) when followed by an adverbial, often in the form of a prepositional phrase or a relative clause. Reference is then to what follows the noun:

[23] The doctor on duty was David Jones.

[24] The doctor who signed the certificate forgot to date it.

(c) when used with a superlative or an ordinal number:

[25] David Jones is the best doctor in the district.

[26] He lives in the third house on the left.

However, the kind of information provided in these examples is still only sufficient to justify the use of *the* if it enables us to identify **exactly** the person or thing referred to. In saying *He was the doctor on duty that evening* we assume there was only one doctor on duty. It would be perfectly correct to say:

[27] David was a doctor on duty that evening.

If we mean that he was **one of those** on duty then. Similarly, we can have *a first prize*, as in

[28] I have taken part in many competitions but have never won a first prize.

On the other hand, any adjective coming before the noun can justify the use of *the* if it enables us to identify the object without doubt. If there are three cups on the table, a white one, a blue one and a brown one, and you ask me which one is mine, either *the white (one), the blue (one)* or *the brown (one)* will give you an **exact** answer.

A slightly different use of *the* occurs in cases like *the law school, the wine trade, the coal industry,* where *law, wine, coal* bear the main stress. A university contains several schools or faculties; *trade* is made up of various trades or branches of commerce; *industry* has its branches too. *The law school, the wine trade,* etc. refer to **one specific** branch of the organisation or activity concerned.

Similarly, with mass nouns we need to know when a noun is sufficiently specified to justify replacing zero by *the.* The mere insertion of an adjective is not enough. Thus, at university we can study art – *classical art* or *modern art;* or *economics* – *nineteenth-century economics,* if we like; *history* – *ancient history, Chinese history, European history* or some other kind. Note that *European history* refers to European history in general, but *the European history we learnt at school* is specified. The same thing applies to unit nouns in the plural; the mere insertion of an adjective does not justify inserting *the.* Thus, we can import bicycles – *British bicycles,* or *Japanese bicycles;* or *glass, Venetian glass, Czech glass* or any other kind. Again, note the difference between *Venetian glass is beautiful* and *The Venetian glass my mother gave me was wonderful.*

3.16 SPECIFICATION BY 'OF' – PHRASES

A phrase beginning with *of* will usually provide sufficient specification to justify the use of *the* before mass nouns or unit nouns in the plural: cp. *Oxford University* but *the University of Oxford.* Similarly, *Chinese history* but *the history of China; nineteenth-century literature* but *the literature of the nineteenth century.*

However, an *of*-phrase need not always attract *the*. Compare *the Peace of Versailles* with *peace of mind* i .e. peace in the mind, mental peace. Compare *the freedom of university life* (as distinct from the restrictions of life at school) with *freedom of speech,* or *freedom to express one's opinions.* Similarly, a relative clause after a mass noun may provide the specification that requires *the*:

> [29] Work can be enjoyable; but the work that factory workers have to do can be very monotonous.

But relative clauses, too, do not always attract *the*. Compare these two:

> [30] I must attend to work that has accumulated while I have been away.

> [31] I must attend to the work that has accumulated etc.

Both are correct: in the first the speaker is referring to work vaguely, while in the second the reference is to certain specific tasks and to those only. It is the intuitive or conscious awareness of such subtleties that helps to give good writing precision.

COMMENTARY AND DISCUSSION POINTS

It is important to realise that the use of articles and determiners is far from obvious, depending on a student's first language. Some languages, Russian for example, manage perfectly well without articles. Other European languages, quite closely associated with English, do not use articles in the same way, so that what is 'obvious' if you are an English native speaker, may be far from obvious to the student.

Have you had experience of students who:
> were not familiar with articles?
> had particular problems with *the*?
> confused *a/an* and *one*?

The most important single concept – or Primary Distinction – is between conceptualising in mass or in units. It is important to realise that it is not particular **words** which are either mass or unit words, but particular **senses** or **meanings** of the word – *stone* v *a stone*. Some of the 'exceptions' which teachers or students think they have found, are neither more nor less than cases of words which are normally used in their mass sense being used with a countable meaning, as a local baker who advertises '*Speciality Breads baked on the premises.*'

Grammatical categories are arbitrary, and do not necessarily translate from language to language. This can be very disconcerting for students, who expect their own language and the language they are learning to work in similar, if not the same, ways. There is a well-known list of words which are normally countable in many European languages but uncountable in English – *advice, furniture, information* etc. How would you deal with these with students – as a detail they need to learn, or part of the general problems discussed in this chapter?

I looked at every book.
"   "   " all the books.
"   "   " each book.

4 Aspects of Quantity

4.1 HOW THE QUANTIFIERS ARE USED

The determiners that indicate aspects of quantity (see 3.1) can be used:

With mass nouns or units plural	With mass only	With units plural only	With units singular
all	a little	both	all
any	much	a few	any
enough		many	each
a lot		several	either
more			every
most			neither
no			no
plenty			some
some			

Some words refer to more than two units, others with two only:

More than two	Two only
all	both (= the two)
every	—
each	each
some	—
any	either
no	neither

(a) All the quantifiers can come directly before a noun, though *a lot* and *plenty* must be followed by *of*.

(b) All the quantifiers except *every* and *no* can be used as pronouns: *Stamps? I haven't any, but George has some. Everyone* can be used as a substitute for *every* + noun; *none* can be used as a substitute for *no* + noun.

(c) All the pronoun forms, i.e. *some, any, everyone, none* etc. can be used as pre-determiners in the construction:

Pre-determiner		Definite identifier	Noun
some, any		the, this, that	money
every one	+ of +	these, those,	books
none		my, your, his etc.	

After *all* and *both*, the *of* can be omitted. After *both*, *the* can also be omitted. We can say *all of those* or *all those* (but only *all of them, all of it*). *All* and *both*, as well as *each*, can also be used in these constructions:

[1]   They all (= all/of them) went home.

[2]   They all have their jobs to do.

[3]   They have all gone.

[4]   They are all here. They are all waiting.

[5]   I have seen them all (= all of them). I have given them all their tickets.

Note the difference between [2], where *have* is a 'full' verb, and [3], where *have* is an auxiliary.

4.2 ALL

Suppose two parcels arrive at my house. One parcel contains a large piece of cake, in a solid mass. It is *a piece of cake,* i.e. part of a greater mass, not an object complete in itself. The other parcel contains books, independent units, each a complete whole.

 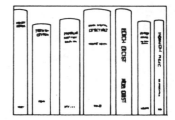

Fig. 7

There we have all the cake and all the books. Note: *All the cake – all of it – is in one box. All the books – all of them – are in another.*

The negative of *all* is *not all*, which may mean *almost all* or *only some*. The opposite of *all* is *none*.

4.3 EVERY

In saying *all the books*, we have in mind a collection of units, with emphasis on the collection. We can imagine the same books and emphasis on the units: in that case, we refer to *every book*, and say *Every book is in the box.*

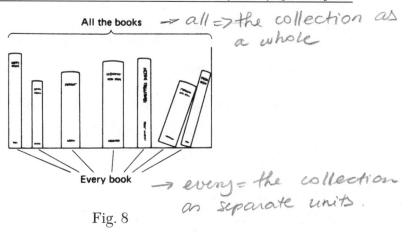

Fig. 8

Then we have *every book* or *every one of them*. **All v every** is a matter of the collection as a whole *v* the collection considered as separate units. The double focus in *every*, i.e. the focus on both the unit separately and the units collectively, often leads to sentences like *Everyone was in their place*, where *their* refers not to one person but to many. *Everyone was in his place*, though traditionally 'correct', can now sound pedantic and even gives offence to some.

4.4 EACH

Consider the books again, not all at once, but one at a time: look at *each book* separately. We could, if space permitted, show each book in a series of diagrams like this.

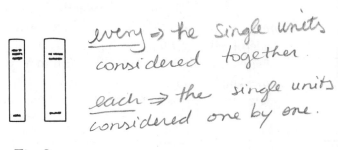

Fig. 9

The contrast in *every v each* is between the single units considered together and the single units considered one by one. The difference between *every* and *each* was well illustrated in a film of Shakespeare's Julius Caesar, in which Mark Antony was addressing the crowd in the market place after Caesar's death. Paraphrasing Shakespeare's words slightly, Antony was declaring: *'Caesar has left to every man his fields'* (the film showed us all the people cheering and looking joyfully at one another) *'and to each'* (pause: the film gave a close-up of one man after another, looking enquiringly and then congratulating himself, as Antony went on) *'a thousand drachmas.'*

Apart from that slight difference in emphasis, *every* and *each* may not only have the same meaning but be interchangeable in sentences on the model of:

[6] Every book (or Each book) was by a well-known author.

However, the two words are not always interchangeable:

(a) Both *every* and *each* could only be used in the example [6] above if there were <u>three books or more</u>: only *each* would be acceptable if there were no more than two.

(b) While we could say *Every one*, or *Each one, was by a well-known author*, <u>we could omit *one* after *each* but not after *every*.</u>

(c) We could not replace *each* by *every* in the sentences:

[7] The books cost two pounds each.

[8] I have given them each their tickets.

Note the concord in these examples:

[9] Each of them has a ticket.

[10] They have each had their tickets.

4.5 ANY

Now suppose I cut the cake into slices, of different sizes, and say to you, '*Take any of it*'; and suppose I offer you the books saying, '*Take any book you like, any one of them, any of them.*' If you take me at my word, you will choose whatever slice of cake or whatever book or as many slices of cake or as many books or whatever kind of book you like. You may, if you are greedy, take everything. I am giving you an <u>*unlimited*</u> choice within the whole <u>range</u>; each part of the cake, each book, stands a chance of being selected, thus:

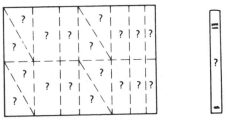 

Fig. 10

So <u>*any*</u> indicates <u>one unit, or one number or part or kind, chosen from all</u>; and we can say *any cake, any of the cake, any of it, any book, any books, any one*;

any two etc. *Any child could tell you that* means that there is not one child in all the world who would fail to tell you; your choice is unlimited.

In *one chosen from all* the emphasis could fall on *one* or on *all*. Hence a statement like *I don't lend my books to any of the students* can be interpreted in two ways. Spoken with strong stress and falling intonation on *any*, it would mean I don't lend my books to one single student (emphasis on *one*) – in fact, I lend them to nobody. Spoken with a fall – rise intonation on *any* and another rise on *students*, it would mean I don't lend my books to one or more of all the students (emphasis on *all*) but only to one or more of a selected few.

4.6 SOME

Instead of giving you an unlimited choice, I can divide the parcels up so as to give you one fixed part of the mass or one fixed number of the units, so that you get *some* /sʌm/ of the cake or *some*/səm/ cake and *some* /sʌm/ of the books or *some* /səm/ books.

Fig. 11

Put a piece of paper over Fig. 11, quickly. Can you say exactly what size that piece of cake is, or how many books I have given you? You will probably guess, and you may guess wrong; but whatever the answer is, only one answer is possible. *Some* indicates a fixed though unstated quantity – **a limited but unspecified amount** of a mass or number of units.

Some is used as a **quantifier**, answering the question *How much?* or *How many?*

As a quantifier, *some* can stand in contrast with *all* or with *none*.

The quantity it refers to is usually small, though it could be fairly large as in

[11] Are we nearly there yet?
    – Oh no, we still have some way to go.

Some can mark a **contrast** between one part of a whole and another, as in

[12] Some people like tea, some prefer coffee, some like plain water.

Some can also be an **identifier**, answering the question *What?* or *Which?* Thus:

[13] What book can I find that information in?
    – I don't know; but there must be some book in the library that will tell you.

Contrast that example with *Any book will tell you* and again the limited choice is apparent.

4.7 SOME V ANY

Some as a quantifier, not *any*, is required in an affirmative statement like

[14] There are some books in my bag. (A fixed though unstated number)

whereas *any* as a quantifier, not *some*, is required in a negative statement like

[15] I haven't any money.

The negative may be contained in a word other than *not*, e.g. *never, hardly (ever), seldom, rarely*, as in

[16] I seldom have any luck in these competitions.

or it can be carried over from a main clause to a subordinate one, as in

[17] I didn't know you had any brothers and sisters.

In questions, *some* can be used, especially if an affirmative answer is expected; or *any*, if the answer is in doubt:

[18] Would you like some more tea?

[19] I can't find the milk. Did we get any today?

Note that *some* but not *any*, as a quantifier, will occur as a single word answer, as in

[20] Is there any bread left?
    – Some/None. (*Any* would be unacceptable here.)

As an identifier, *any* can always be used in an affirmative statement, as in

[21] Any child can tell you that.

4.8 No, None, Not Any

Finally, when every piece of the cake is eaten and every book is given away (notice that I said *every* there, since my emphasis is on all the units considered together), then I have *no cake, no book* or *no books* left – I have *none*. Alternatively, we could say, *I haven't any cake, I haven't a book or any books – I haven't any left*. *N't any* would be more informal than *no*. While the unit noun after *no* may be singular or plural, singular is usual in a case like

[22] There's no telephone in my office.

i.e. when we would expect to find at least one telephone; and plural would occur in a case like

[23] That poor child has no shoes.

i.e. when more than one shoe would be natural. *None* meaning 'not one of them' is subject to the same kind of double focus as *every*. Though *None of them remains*, with a singular verb, is 'correct', *None of the students have remembered to bring their books* would be normal and acceptable in conversational style.

4.9 Everything, Anything, Something, Nothing

Every (not *each*), *any, some* and *no* can combine with *one, body, thing* and *where* to produce *everyone, everybody* etc. Each of these combinations would be written as one word, except *no one*. Note that *every* etc. plus *other thing, other person, other place* are usually replaced by *everything else*, etc. What has been said of the difference between *some* and *any* would also apply to the difference between *something* and *anything* and often compounds. Thus:

[24] I have something to tell you.

[25] I haven't anything to say.

[26] What would you like to eat?
    – Something light.
    – Nothing, thank you.
    – Anything.

In the response, *Anything* cannot refer to quantity but has a meaning similar to that of *any* in example [21].

4.10 (A) Little, (A) Few

(A) little and *(a) few*, can be considered as aspects of *some*, with emphasis on the smallness of the amount *(little)* or of the number *(few)*. *A little* and *a few*

suggest a **positive** quantity – more than none, while *little* and *few* suggest a **negative** one, almost none.

The pattern is similar to that of *to, at, from* (See section 27, page 23).

```
0  1  2  3  4  5  etc.
    ──────────────▶        a little, a few
None      x                some
    ◀──────────────        little, few
```

Thus:

[27] Don't hurry. We've a little time, a few minutes, yet.

[28] He rarely speaks. He has little to say. He is a man of few words.

Though *(a) few, fewer, fewest,* refer to number (of units), not amount (mass), *less* is becoming increasingly used in everyday speech instead of *fewer,* as in

[29] There were less than fifty people present.

In any case, *less* would be normal when reference is being made to a sum of money or a distance as in:

[30] This suit cost less than twenty pounds.

[31] Our house is less than a hundred metres from the station.

4.11 MUCH, MANY

The distinction between amount (mass) and number (units) is clearly made by *much* and *many*:

[32] How much bread have we got?
   – Not much.
   – Too much.
   – Not so much as yesterday.

[33] How many potatoes are there?
   – Not many.
   – Too many.
   – Not so many etc.

While in short affirmative answers to those questions, the responder can say *Too much* or *Too many*, we would not hear *We've got much*: instead *(We've got) a lot* or *plenty* or *a good deal* would be normal. *There are many* would be more acceptable than **There's much*; but, even so, *There are a lot* or *plenty* or *a good many* would be more idiomatic. However, affirmative *much* and *many*, not modified by *too* or *so*, would be perfectly all right in more formal style, as in *There is much to be said for this proposal.*

4.12 BOOK AS A MASS, CAKE AS A UNIT; ALL v WHOLE

The two parcels (in 4.2) might have contained one large book and a box of small cakes. We can then say:

all (of) the book	all (of) the cakes
—	every or each cake
any of the book	any (single) cake, any cakes
some of the book	some of the cakes
none of the book	none of the cakes
much of the book	many of the cakes
a little of the book	a few of the cakes

[34] I haven't read all (of) the book (or the whole book) yet.

[35] Have you understood any of the book?
   – I've understood a little of it, but not much.

Note also that *little* in *a little cake* can be either an adjective, meaning *small* (one little cake) or a determiner, meaning *a small quantity of* as in *May I have a little (of that) cake, please?*

Before certain nouns referring to periods of time, not only *of* but also *the* may be omitted after *all*, as in *We travelled all day and all night.* Note the difference between *all day* (i.e. the whole day) and *every day* (all the days in a limited or unlimited period). *All morning, all evening, all week* are also frequently used.

4.13 BOTH, EITHER, NEITHER

The distinction between *both*, meaning *the two*, and *all*, presents no difficulty. But as *any* presents such a constant problem, it is helpful to see it in contrast with *either*, thus:

[36] You can't have either of these two books – not this, nor that one.

[37] You can't have any of these three (four, five) etc. – not this, nor that, nor that and so on.

[38] Either of these two roads will take you to London.

[39] Any of these three (etc.) will take you there.

Similarly, *none* can be seen in contrast with *neither* (where the same option between singular and plural verb is open):

[40] Neither of the two men was (or were) present.

[41] None of the three (etc.) was (or were).

COMMENTARY AND DISCUSSION POINTS

It is worth noticing again that Close draws attention to abstract, underlying distinctions of meaning. No amount of explaining away the use of forms will ever tackle the real problems of English grammar. He emphasises, again and again, that the choice of language item is dependent both upon the real world – the **objective** situation – and on the way the speaker perceives the situation at the moment of speaking – a **subjective** view. This point is sometimes lost on students who want a decisive answer to questions such as *Should I say ... or ...?* They are frequently unhappy with the answer *It depends what you mean*, but frequently this is the only possible answer.

Part of a well-designed language teaching programme will, from time to time remind students that grammar is not a set of arbitrary rules, but is about **meaning.** This point can never be emphasised enough.

Can you find an example in this chapter which would help you to remind students of the importance of the speaker's own perception in choosing a particular language form?

5 **The Tenses**

5.1 ASPECTS OF ACTIVITY

In what are generally called the tenses, we are concerned with aspects of activity and of time. Time itself might be regarded as an aspect of activity, insofar as it is only in terms of events that time can be measured.

English-speakers see activity from several points of view. To understand its expression in the English verb system, we must think of:

(a) the general idea of an act, not containing any of the distinctions referred to in the rest of this paragraph

(b) the act seen as accomplished and as a completed whole

(c) the act seen as uncompleted, as having begun and being still in progress. The difference between (b) and (c) is therefore comparable to that between *all* and *some*.

(d) the act performed once

(e) the act performed repeatedly; a whole series of acts, the series seen as a whole

(f) a partial, uncompleted series of acts; the acts being performed temporarily rather than permanently

Here is an example of each:

(a) [1] Tell a lie? That's something he would never do.

(b) [2] I tell you it's true. (I tell you, definitely, now.)

(c) [3] Listen carefully to what I'm telling you. (Listen while the telling is in progress; I haven't finished yet.)

(d) [4] I see a ship.

(e) [5] I see my neighbour on the train every day.

(f) [6] I'm playing tennis every day this week. (partial series)
    – But you're always playing tennis. (series never stops)

You will see that the continuous is used in examples [3] and [6].

(a) We can compare the general idea of the act with the general concept referred to by a noun as in 3.2 where the zero article is required.

(b) The act seen as a whole could be illustrated like this:

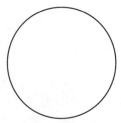

Fig. 12

(c) The action in progress, like this:

Fig. 13

There, the thin line represents time, the thicker line represents action in progress: this is the continuous, expressed by *be* + the *-ing* form of the verb.

(d) The act performed once, like this:

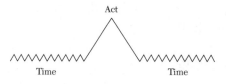

Fig. 14

(e) A series of acts, viewed as a whole, thus:

Fig. 15

This can be compared with the illustration for *every* in 4.3.

(f) A partial or uncompleted series of acts, like this:

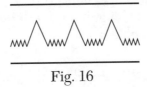

Fig. 16

and an uncompleted series never stopping, like this:

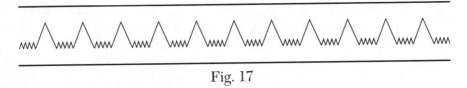

Fig. 17

This is, again, continuous aspect, expressed by *be + -ing*.

Another way of illustrating these aspects of activity would be as follows, using *I go* as an example:

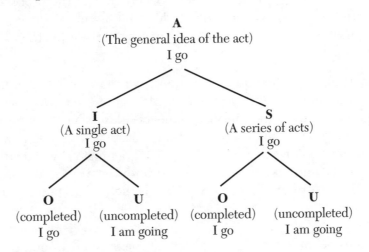

Fig 18

In figure 18:

A represents the general concept

I the single act   **S** the series

I O the single act completed   **SO** the series completed

I U the single act uncompleted   **SU** the series uncompleted

Note that *I go* is used for the whole scheme except **I U** and **S U**: in other words, we say *I go* until and unless we are concerned with the **uncompleted** act or series, when we can use *I am going*, if it is on **the act, or series, in progress** that we wish to place our emphasis.

I repeat 'until and unless we are concerned with' that aspect. What is important is not so much the **objective** fact as the aspect of the fact that the speaker has in mind and wishes to express. For example:

(a) In saying *I read in bed for half an hour before I turn out the light,* I refer to a series (of acts) which happens to be incomplete, insofar as I have not given up the habit of reading in bed; but it is not that fact that I wish to emphasise. I am viewing the series as a whole without wishing to draw attention to the idea of the incompleteness of the series. Similarly, in *The River Danube flows into the Black Sea,* we are not concerned with the fact that the Danube is in process of flowing or that it never stops. We could be so concerned and say *The Danube is flowing unusually fast today* or *It is for ever flowing and emptying its waters into the sea.* In *The Danube flows etc.*, we see the **phenomenon as a whole** without those particular distinctions.

(b) In saying *I'm telling you* in [3], I am concerned with the process of telling and with the incompletion of it. My telling may (or may not) be accomplished. If it is, that is irrelevant and is not the aspect to which I want to draw your attention.

(c) In reporting two uncompleted actions, we may wish to emphasise the progress of one but not of the other. *As I stand here, the procession is entering the hall.* It would be vain of me, besides giving the impression that the procession was small and its entrance hasty, if I said *As I am standing here, the procession enters the hall,* though grammatically that is not wrong. Both verbs could take the **O** form and both the **U** in that sentence. But notice the first example given, which is an actual quotation from a radio commentary.

Note that the uncompleted act may eventually be finished, or not. In saying *I'm putting my pen on the desk,* i.e. in describing an action in progress, not stating my intention, I ought to be concentrating on the gradual movement of hand and pen through the air before they have reached the desk. They may get there, or they may not. It happens to be in my power to stop them. **I U** can therefore be easily applied to a voluntary act.

It may be convenient to teach beginners that the difference between *I'm going* and *I go* is that the former refers to an act performed at the time of speaking, the latter to the act performed habitually. Unfortunately, the difference between *I go,* as an expression of **I O**, and *I'm going,* as an expression of **S U**, is also that *I go* in that sense refers to an act performed at the time of speaking, while *I'm going* can refer to habitual action. Admittedly, there are many examples of **I U** in which the predominant idea is one of 'activity now', for example:

[7]   (I can't understand you) – Are you trying to speak English?

Examples of this kind could be compared with ones in which the predominant idea is that of the act performed habitually:

[8]   Do you speak English at home?

In those examples, the change of verb form makes it clear that in *Are you trying* I mean **at this moment**, while in *Do you speak* I mean **usually**. But in linking an example of the continuous with *at this moment*, and an example of the simple present with *usually* and generalising accordingly, we are reasoning from only part of the evidence. It is quite possible to say, as I do now:

[9]   I stop work at this moment – I'm usually feeling pretty tired by this hour of night.

The difference between momentary action and habitual activity is indeed expressed in English by a change of verb form, but only incidentally in certain types of usage. The difference may be underlined by adverbial expressions such as *at this moment*, or *regularly, often, sometimes, always*. *Now* is not a good example of such an adverb since it can be used for regular activity as well as momentary action, completed as well as uncompleted, e.g.

[10] Now I put down my pen. **IO**

[11] Now I am looking out of the window. **IU**

[12] Now I write all my letters myself; I used to dictate them. **SO**

[13] Now I am writing twenty pages a day – last year I could only do six. **SU**

It can also be used with the past tense and with apparent reference to the future:

[14] I saw him just now. Now we'll make some progress!.

5.2 Physical and Mental Activity, Sensory and Mental Perception

Just as some of the things we talk about can be imagined more easily in the mass than as units, and vice versa (see 3.8), so some of our actions are more easily imagined as completed acts than as uncompleted processes. On the other hand, the uncompleted state is more easily imagined with some actions than with others. A commentator on the football match saw the game as a series of accomplished acts:

> [15] Johnson passes to Roberts, Roberts to Watkins, Watkins takes it forward, oh he slips past the centre half beautifully, he shoots ...

– all perfect examples of **I O**. Watching a boat race, the commentator is, by the nature of the event, more conscious of movement in progress:

> [16] Oxford are rowing splendidly one two three four—they're just coming in sight of Hammersmith Bridge. Ah—Cambridge are increasing their pace

– all **I U**. Here the reader must again be warned against generalising from incidental factors. The movements of football may be quicker, those of rowing may take longer; but the essential factors determining the usage of the verb-form is not speed, or length of duration, but rather the fact that the speed makes the spectator more aware of the completed act, the duration more aware of the action in progress.

Verbs referring to physical activity, [17], or to mental activity [18], to physical sensation [19], or to a process that can last a considerable time, [20] and thus have duration, are often used in **I U**:

> [17] (Please be quiet.) I'm writing an important letter.

> [18] I'm considering whether to phone instead.

> [19] My head is aching terribly.

> [20] You're getting tired.

We can easily imagine ourselves in the middle of the act of writing a letter. We can stop the action, and leave it uncompleted, whenever we like. It is therefore a good idea to introduce continuous aspect with verbs of that kind. On the other hand, it is not easy to imagine ourselves in the middle of the act of closing a book, switching on a light or opening a door. That is why I said earlier that *I'm opening the door*, as a commentary on an action performed at the time of speaking, is unnatural. With verbs like *open (a door)*, *switch on (a light)*, *hit*, *jump, bark* and so on, the continuous aspect only makes sense if one is referring to repeated acts of opening, switching, hitting, etc.

Similarly, it is difficult (though for a scientist not impossible) to catch oneself in the middle of a single act of *seeing* or *hearing*. *To see* or *to hear* is to receive a sensory impression. The reception of the impression is an involuntary act: we cannot normally prevent the completion of it. Thus, as we commonly say in English, *you see – or you don't (see)*. Yet sometimes it is possible for us to perceive the reception of a visual image in an unfinished state. Wearing the wrong spectacles or having dined not wisely but too well, *I might be seeing double*. Such occurrences of *see* in **I U** may be rare, but they help to explain why *see* is normally found only in the completed aspect. Yet in **S U** *see* would occur as frequently as any other verb, since we have no difficulty in imagining an uncompleted series of the acts of perception:

[21] 'I'm seeing too many pictures,' said Sue at the exhibition. 'I can't look at any more.'

In contrast with *seeing*, the voluntary act of *looking (at something)* is easy to imagine in **I U**. Looking at something is like focusing a camera. It can go on for some time: it is physical activity having duration. Seeing something is more like taking a snapshot; once we have pressed the button, we cannot stop the shutter opening and leaving an impression on the film.

Parallel with *see* v *look (at)* is *hear* v *listen (to)*. *Smell, taste* and *feel* can express both voluntary action and sensory impression and correspond with both *look (at)* and *see* accordingly, as in:

[22] Why are you feeling the radiators?
– To see if the heating is on. I feel rather cold. Yes. The radiator feels quite cold (i.e. I feel cold when I touch it).

When we feel cold, we receive an impression through the senses. When we know what the temperature is, we register a mental impression; and that experience, too, is difficult to imagine in its uncompleted state. We can *be finding out* what the temperature is; but, again, **we either know, or we don't**. *Know, remember, forget, think, believe, suppose, want, like, love, doubt, hope, wish,* are therefore, like *see* and *hear,* very unlikely to occur in the continuous aspect. Note the difference between each member of the following pairs:

[23] Please be quiet. I'm thinking. (mental activity)
I think you're right. (mental impression)
[24] The jury is considering its verdict. (mental activity)
We consider the prisoner guilty. (mental impression)

Here, teachers must distinguish between helpful advice and absolute statement. They would be justified in advising pupils not to use *know, remember,* etc. in the *-ing* form of the verb until they are more advanced. They would be wrong in making them learn a 'rule' to the effect that these words are not used in the continuous form at all. Just as all nouns in English can, potentially, fill all the six positions in 3.8, so all full verbs can, potentially, fill all the positions in Figure 18.

5.3 Psychological Subtleties

Since we are concerned in this book with the connection between grammatical form and what we have in mind, it is not surprising that in many of the problems we are discussing there are psychological subtleties. Students can fairly easily understand the difference between *I'm thinking* (mental activity) and *I think* (mental impression). They may be more puzzled to hear *I'm thinking you're right*. That can be perfectly 'correct' if the speaker is deliberately using the marked form to suggest that a certain conclusion is forming itself in his or her mind but is not yet final. Thus *I think you're right* is more definite (besides being safer for the student to imitate) than *I'm thinking you're right*. Similarly, *I'm liking my work*, instead of the normal and more decided *I like it*, suggests that the process of becoming adjusted to it is still going on; or it might mean that I am lingering over its delights. Then consider the difference between the following:

[25] (a) I hope you will come and have lunch with me.
(b) I am hoping you will come and have lunch with me.

Both are right but they are not equal in the effect they might have on the hearer. Native speakers who select one rather than the other, may be quite unaware that they do, and unable to explain why they do. Any explanation one can offer might be drawn from purely personal associations. My own explanation is that a busy, self-important man might feel (a) to be too presumptuous, and refuse the invitation, but (b) flatteringly deferential and accept; while someone else to whom that invitation was given might feel (a) to be definitely meant, and accept with pleasure, but (b) to be uncertain and not sufficiently pressing. The speaker's attitude — dictatorial or deferential, positive or uncertain—can be an important factor in these cases. However, the basic factor in the above examples is not the positiveness, the uncertainty, or whatever it may be in the speaker's attitude, but the speaker's conception of the action as a whole, as accomplished (*hope*), or partial, in progress or continuing (*hoping*).

I am leaving tomorrow

One such subtlety that has become stereotyped and commonly adopted is the use of the uncompleted aspect to indicate action which is about to begin or is due to take place in the future. Thus *we're starting* can mean either that action has begun and is in progress, or that action is about to begin or has been arranged, that the required impetus has been given, so that the process has in a sense begun already. Note:

[26] I am leaving the country tomorrow and will be abroad for six weeks.

This example provides a contrast between (*am*) (*leav*)*ing* and *will* + infinitive, and we must discuss this later both as an aspect of time (Futures, page 77) and as a question of mood (Chapter 6). It illustrates an aspect of activity insofar as it suggests and emphasises the idea that I have, or someone else has, arranged that I shall leave the country, and the process has in that sense begun, though I do not see it yet as completed—in fact, it may not **be** completed. Note that the terse, businesslike speaker might see the act as completed, and announce firmly *I fly to New York tomorrow*; or, like Julius Caesar, *Tomorrow I cross the Rubicon*. The **O** form can also be used when the speaker's plans are determined by external arrangements: *According to schedule, I leave at seven in the morning.*

As we are seldom so confident that the future will be fulfilled, the **U** form is commoner than the **O** form when the present tense-form is used with future reference. Yet either may occur in the same situation. Referring to future time, one can say *The ship sails at three* (**I O**) or *The ship is sailing at three* (**I U**). It is commonly believed that the latter way of referring to the future is restricted to verbs indicating movement from one place to another. It occurs frequently as an indication of a planned movement; but it can be applied to any situation subject to human control; e.g. *We're discussing your case on Friday* (that item is already on the agenda of our meeting). However, we could not say **I'm sneezing in a moment* or **It is raining tomorrow*, since sneezing and raining are not subject to human planning. Moreover, *I'm knowing the result tomorrow* would be rare, such an act of perception being difficult to imagine in an uncompleted state. Nevertheless, we can say *I'm seeing the doctor on Tuesday* (i.e. I have made an appointment and the process has therefore begun). With acts of perception the **O** form is possible, provided such acts are subject to plan, e.g. *We hear the results tomorrow* (that is when they are due to be published).

I am going to leave tomorrow

We frequently find the pattern *(I am) going to (leave) (tomorrow)*, especially in spoken English. If the essential factor in the *(I am leav)ing* pattern is the idea that a process has started in the sense that some event has been planned, the essential factor in the *(I am) going to (leave)* pattern is a focus on some **present** factor which the speaker feels certain will lead to a future event. The 'present factor' can be decision, intention or preparation, or it can be an obvious symptom of what the future will bring. The *(I am) going to (leave)* pattern allows the speaker to state separately the preparation for the event and its possible accomplishment. Note how accomplishment is expressed by the infinitive, *to leave*, see Chap. 8. The accomplishment, of course, is imagined, not actual, and may not result. Examples:

[27] I am going to write to him soon.

[28] You're going to break that chair if you're not careful.

The speaker sees signs of what will happen and is sure of the result. You do not intend to break the chair, and no one has arranged that you will do so: *You're breaking* would therefore be wrong in this context.

[29] I'm going to sneeze in a moment. (The signs are clear – I know what will happen.)

[30] It's going to rain this evening.

[31] We're going to understand this eventually.

It will be seen from examples [28], [29], [30] and [31] that the *going to leave* pattern can be used when the present continuous pattern cannot. This may explain the very frequent use in conversation of the former, which is often chosen mechanically when the latter would be equally acceptable. The question of *am leaving/am going to leave* v *future* will be discussed on page 77ff. Meanwhile, *am leaving (tomorrow)* v *am going to leave* could be expressed as **process imagined as begun** (in the sense that preliminary decisions, plans or arrangements have been made) v **present factors**, (personal intentions or objective symptoms, imagined as leading to a completed act).

5.4 ASPECTS OF TIME

I O, **I U**, **S O** and **S U** can be combined with nine aspects of time, and the resultant combinations are expressed in the various tense forms. Aspects of time depend on the speaker's point of primary concern (SPPC) in the natural order of events, and on the direction of the speaker's vision from the standpoint adopted.

We might illustrate the natural order of events by a row of numbers, as on the scoreboard for the game of billiards:

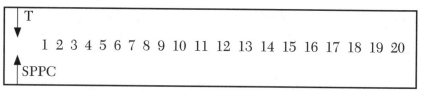

Fig. 19

The arrows on the scoreboard move horizontally and mark the scores of the two players or teams. Let us suppose that the numbers represent happenings, that the top arrow is Time (T) and the bottom the speaker's point of primary concern (SPPC). T moves regularly forward, as if by clockwork. SPPC may keep pace with it, be behind it, or in front of it. T remains pointing vertically downwards. SPPC can swing like the needle of an electrical instrument, so as to point backwards or forwards, at any angle, from whatever position it occupies.

1 UNLIMITED TIME: PRESENT TENSE

In the first aspect of time, the 'game' has not begun and neither of the arrows is 'in play'. Time, here, is unlimited; undivided; or it does not matter; we are concerned with **timelessness.**

[32] The sea breaks eternally onto the shore. (**O**)

[33] The earth is constantly revolving on its axis. (**U**)

Breaks and *is revolving* are in the present tense. We regard all time as present until we feel the need to mark some of it off as past or yet to come.

2 PRESENT TIME: PRESENT TENSE

The second aspect is present time as distinct from past or future. Here the arrows have moved into play and the scores are equal.

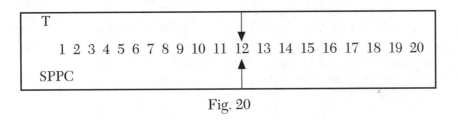

Fig. 20

The speaker's attention is focused on an action performed at the time when (s)he is commenting on it. SPPC can be pointing straight towards T, in which case the speaker is commenting on something happening at the very moment of utterance:

[34] A. Watch me. I put a cross here. X (**I O**)
     B. I'm watching you. What are you doing that for? (**I U**)

B is continuing to watch A to see what A will do next. SPPC can also swing backwards and forwards so as to cover a range of activity and events both before and after T. The speaker is then considering something that has actually happened as well as something that (s)he imagines will take place. Thus:

[35] My sister lives in England. (**I O**)

[36] I usually get up at seven. (**S O**)

[37] I am learning Arabic. (**I U**)

[38] I'm getting up at six this week to revise for my exam. (**S U**)

SPPC can swing so far backwards and forwards that it can cover an unlimited range, which is what we have in Unlimited Time (1 above). But the range we are concerned with here is limited, though not necessarily defined: it is **Now** as distinct from **Then** (past) and **Then** (future).

The previous paragraph could be summarised in this way:

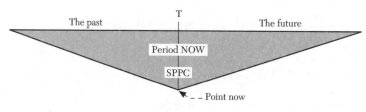

Fig. 21

The horizontal line corresponds with the row of numbers in Fig. 20; the vertical line with the line made by the two arrows. The shaded part of Fig. 21 represents the present period: its limits can be close together or far apart. They can be so close as to meet at the **Point Now**, the momentary present. Or they can extend on either side of the **Point Now** so that the **Period Now** overlaps with both past and future. Thus, while the events in example [34] take place at the **Point Now**, those in [35]-[38] are true of part of the past and of the future, and may be true of the present moment. Whether the speaker's attention is focused on **Point Now** or **Period Now**, the Present tense is appropriate.

3   PRE-PRESENT TIME: PRESENT PERFECT

The third aspect of time is pre-present, leading up to the present moment. Here, SPPC is still at the same point as T; but while the T arrow remains pointing vertically downwards, the SPPC arrow points backwards into pre-present time. In other words, the speaker is concerned with a period of time **before and ending at point now**. The speaker is not concerned with a **specified** time before now; if that were the case, SPPC would be behind T, not level with it. The pre-present may begin anywhere in the past, no matter how long ago. However, the speaker has a natural tendency to give more attention to that part of the period which is nearest the present, that is to the recent past: hence the darker shading in Fig. 22 below. The beginning of the pre-present period may or may not be mentioned: it is often marked by *since*, as in *We've been here since Friday*. This aspect of time is called the perfective and the verb form that expresses it is called the Present Perfect.

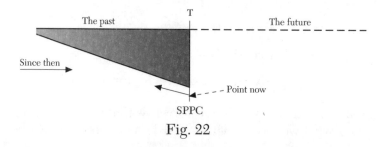

Fig. 22

We can move the SPPC arrow in different ways. Either it can point vaguely towards some time within the pre-present, in which case the speaker is concerned with activity occurring at some unspecified time before now. Or it can move progressively from a backward-pointing position to a completely vertical one, in which case the speaker is concerned with activity continuing throughout the pre-present period till now. In either case, **it is the pre-present period that is the speaker's basic interest;** and it is this that determines the use of the Present Perfect. As the Present Perfect is not concerned with specified past time, it is not normally used with past time adverbials (e.g. *yesterday, last year*); though it can naturally be used with *till now, by now, so far* and the more formal *hitherto*. Occasional examples of Present Perfect with past time adverbials do occur. Students are advised to avoid this unusual use.

Here are some examples showing different sub-categories of the basic pre-present:

(a) Activity at unspecified time before now

[39] – Have you ever been to Mexico (at any time, yet)?
     – Yes, I've been there once (time unspecified). (**I O**)
     – I've never had a chance to go yet.

Note the use of *yet* with the Present Perfect in questions and in the negative; and the use of *ever*, meaning at any time. The scope of *ever*, like that of *any*, is unlimited: the limited but unspecified *once* could be compared with *some* (4.6).

[40] Do you know this village?
     – I know it well. I've lived here. (**I O**)

Note that the second speaker in [39] is not in Mexico; and in [40] no longer lives in that village.

[41] Why are your hands so dirty?
     – I've been working in the garden. (**I U**)

[42] Who is that man? I've seen him several times. (**S O**)

[43] You wouldn't recognise Athens now. They've been building blocks of flats everywhere. (**S U**)

(b) Activity continuing till now

[44] I've lived here since 1984 – for the last twelve years. (**I O**)

Compare [44] with [40]. The addition of *since 1984* (i.e. from that point of time in the past) and *for the last twelve years* (i.e. throughout that period) implies that my living here has continued till now and I live here still. But even if I am living here still, I do not use the Present tense in [44], nor in [45], [46], [47], because in those examples I am **primarily concerned with occurrences within the pre-present period**.

[45] I've been learning Arabic for six months. (**I U**)

[46] I've always got up at seven (and still do). (**S O**)

[47] I've been playing tennis every day this week so far. (**S U**)

Note the emphasis on the last phase of the pre-present in

[48] I've just finished another page.

Action completed before now will generally produce effects that are noticeable now, e.g.

[49] You do look clean.
    – Yes, I've just had a hot bath.

However, to understand how the Present Perfect operates – students must consider the aspect of time described above and Fig. 22 and not assume that we use the Present Perfect simply because a result is evident. If they start from that assumption, they will soon discover

(a) that the Present Perfect is used when there is no result at all and even when a noticeable result is contrary to what might have been expected, as in

[50] Look at you! You've just had a bath and now you're filthy.

(b) that present evidence may be associated with a tense form other than the Present Perfect:

[51] Here are the burglar's footmarks—he came into the house through that window.

Uncompleted action in the pre-present period might (a) be interrupted before now; or (b) continue until now; or (c) being uncompleted, continue through the present. Thus, applying Fig. 13 to Fig. 22, we have

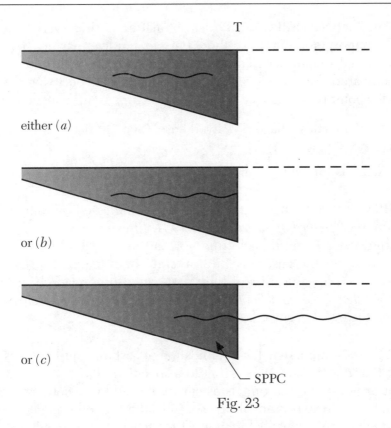

either (*a*)

or (*b*)

or (*c*)

SPPC

Fig. 23

Examples:

(a) [52] Who has been sitting in my chair (and is no longer in it)?

  [53] It's been raining, but it's stopped now.

(b) [54] I'll take the wheel now—you've been driving for four hours.

(c) [55] We've been learning English for ten years (and are learning it still).

In any case, in (a), (b) or (c), what the speaker is primarily concerned with is the action in progress before now, i.e. in the shaded part of Fig. 22.

4   PAST TIME: PAST TENSE

For the fourth aspect of time, marked by the past tense, the speaker's primary concern is with some specific point or period in past time. SPPC is then somewhere behind T, like this:

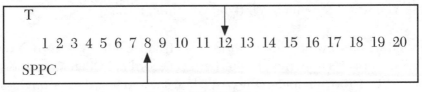

Fig. 24

The distance between SPPC and T does not matter: it can be very great or very small. The important thing is that there is a gap, however narrow, between the two. The move from unspecified time before now to a specific time in the past can be compared with the move from unspecifying *a* to specifying *the* (3.6). A shift of viewpoint from unspecified to specified time is often made in English.

[56] A. I know this village. I've lived here. (See [40].)

   B. Oh, when was that?

   A. It was fifteen years ago.

When SPPC is in time past, the fact is usually indicated by some adverbial expression, e.g. *yesterday, last year, in 1984, fifteen years ago. Ago* marks a time in the past measured back from now, a time that becomes SPPC. *Ago* therefore requires the Past tense, just as *since* in example [44] required the Present Perfect. Specification of time past can also be made by a temporal clause, e.g. *when I was at school*, or by some other device that helps to fix the time when the event occurred.

The Past tense is thus a signal of specification of past time, just as *the* is a signal meaning that the speaker is referring to a specified object (3.6). But though the point or period in past time is usually indicated by something such as an adverb in the context, it is not always so. Consider the following episode from real life. One morning, just before it was time for my family to get up, my wife and I both heard a sound as of footsteps going downstairs. We asked each other, 'What was that?' both thinking of the noise we had heard a moment before. A minute later our son Peter appeared at the door of our room with the newspaper. My wife and I spoke simultaneously:

Myself: Oh, it's you. Good, you've brought the paper.

My wife: Oh, it's you. You went down for the paper.

I used the Present Perfect, my wife the Past. Both were 'right' in the circumstances. But there is a difference in meaning insofar as there was a difference in our points of view, and this would have become apparent had our talk proceeded, as it well might have done, thus:

Wife (to me): All you think about is your newspaper.

Self: You worry too much. Who did you think it was?

Chiefly interested in the paper before me, I had made the **Point Now** my primary concern and used the Present Perfect accordingly. Peter's mother, with her mind still on the moment in the past when she had heard steps on the stairs, had made **that**, a **Point Then**, her primary concern.

That discussion should explain:

> [57] Who broke the window?

The speaker has registered the fact that now it is broken, but is no longer interested in **Now**. What the speaker wants to know is how the accident happened **when** it happened.

> [58] Did you have a good journey? (I'm glad to see you—you know that. I am now thinking of the time in the past when you were on your way here.)

In both those cases, Present Perfect would be equally acceptable: *Oh, who has broken the window?* (I don't want to know how it happened; the fact is that it is broken, and I'm asking who is responsible.) Similarly, with *today, this morning, this afternoon,* etc., both the Past tense (*it happened*) and the Present Perfect (*it has happened*) are possible, according to whether SPPC is **Point Now** or an earlier time, a **Point Then**. Contrast the Present Perfect of [59] and [60] with the past simple for the other two examples.

> [59] Have you been very busy today? (during the period before now).

> [60] I have seen him this morning. I've just seen him.
> (at an unspecified time).

> [61] Your letter reached me this morning. It arrived just now.
> (Someone brought it at a definite moment earlier in the morning; or this morning if the morning has passed.)

> [62] It was terribly hot in town today. (but it is cooler out here in the country, now).

Notice how the Present Perfect and the Past tense are used with *since*:

> [63] Since I heard her sing, I have always admired her.

> [64] Since he was in the army, he has been in much better health.

> [65] Since we have lived here, we have made many friends.

> [66] Since he has been in the army, we have seen him only twice.

In [63], *I heard* occurred at a point of past time which marks the beginning of the pre-present period; and in [64], he was in the army during a period of past time, since when he has been in better health. In [65] and [66] our living here and his being in the army extend throughout the whole pre-present period. The Present Perfect can only be used in a *since* clause with verb referring to activity that can continue throughout a period of time.

As in [62] the Past tense can, but does not necessarily, indicate that former conditions no longer exist. Thus *He was an excellent chairman* suggests that he is not chairman now. *He was a wonderful man* suggests he is dead. Other examples: *Where were you born? I was born at. . .*; and *We enjoyed our stay* immensely (our stay ended, say, yesterday), but *We have enjoyed our stay* (which is now ending).

The difference between the pre-present and the past is thus a matter of **unspecified time before now v specified time in the past, detached from the present;** and the Past tense could be illustrated like this:

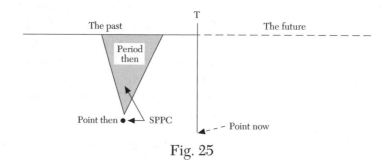

Fig. 25

The **Point Then** or **Period Then** can move forwards as a series of events is reported, e.g. *Caesar came, (then) he saw, (then) he conquered.*

I O, I U, S O, and **S U** (see Fig. 18) can be applied to the Past tense as to the Present. **I O** can be, and often is applied to a single act in past time; **S O** to a series of acts or to past habit; **I U** to uncompleted action; and **S U** to a partial series of acts:

Events occurring at a point of time

> [67] The accident happened at 10.15 this morning. (**I O**)

> [68] Several people were standing there at the time. (**I U**)

Events occurring throughout a period

> [69] I lived in England when I was a boy. (**I O**)

> [70] I got up early in those days. (**S O**)

> [71] I was having breakfast (when he arrived). (**I U**)

> [72] I was getting up at six o'clock every day to prepare for my exams. (**S U**)

I O extending over a period, and **S O**, as in examples [69] and [70], can be expressed by *used to*, when emphasis falls on the idea of an act continued or repeated over a period in the past, but not in the present:

[73] I used to live in England. (but I don't now)

[74] I used to get up early. (now I'm not so energetic)

This emphatic marking would normally only occur once in a short sentence:

[75] I used to get up early when I went to school.

Nor would it occur when the length of duration of the past habit is specified: thus, *used to go* could not replace *went* in *I went swimming every day for six years*, but it could replace *went* in *I went swimming every day*.

5   PRE-PAST TIME: PAST PERFECT

In our fifth aspect of time, the pre-past, SPPC in Fig. 25 is now pointing backwards, and the pattern in Fig. 22 is applied to Fig. 25, thus:

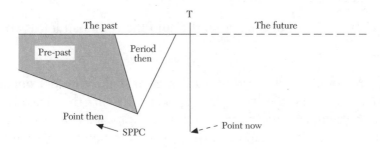

Fig. 26

Activity before then

[76] I hear you went to India last year. Had you ever been there before?
    – Yes, I'd been there six years before. (**I O**)

[77] The streets were so wet, that I naturally supposed it had been raining. (**I U**)

[78] The door-bell rang, but there was nobody there. That had already happened twenty times during the day. (**S O**)

[79] The place looked very different. They had been building everywhere.(**S U**)

Activity continuing till then

[80] I sold my house last summer. I had lived in it for twelve years, ever since my father died. (**I O**)

[81] By the time I arrived in Egypt, I had been studying Arabic for eighteen months. (**I U**)

[82] Till then, I had usually got up at seven; but . . . (**S O**)

[83] I had been getting up at six in order to work at the language, so I arrived rather tired. (**S U**)

In this aspect we are dealing with a prelude to the past and not merely with a sequence of past events. In *Caesar came, (then) he saw, (then) he conquered* SPPC moves forward with each event: one event may precede another, but that is not the **essential** point in the pre-past. This aspect is only adopted when the speaker has to make it clear, or wishes to emphasise the fact, that some action **preceded** SPPC. Thus, in example [80] *I had lived* is necessary to make it clear that the speaker is referring to the period prior to the sale, which is the SPPC; but where my father's death occurs in that order of events is obvious without the particular distinction made by the Past Perfect, hence *my father died*. Other examples:

[84] The train left before I got to the station.

The order of events is clear. To emphasise it, I could say *the train had left*; but it would be pedantic to regard *the train left* as 'wrong'.

[85] When I arrived at the station I found the train had left (two minutes before).

Here *had left* would be required to make it clear that the train's departure on that occasion preceded my arrival, and especially to mark the idea of such-and-such a time **before**. *I found the train left two minutes before*, could mean that it usually left, or was scheduled to leave, two minutes before the time I arrived.

[86] 'As the Chairman told you, I was in Ghana,' the lecturer began.

The speaker's being in Ghana preceded the Chairman's remarks. However, not only is the order of events obvious to the audience, but the speaker's primary concern is with her stay in Ghana, and it is this that she is going to talk about.

[87] I saw Michael on Sunday. He hadn't gone back to the office yet.

Here, *he hadn't gone back* is essential to the sense. *He didn't go back* would suggest that his non-return was the consequence of my seeing him; in any case, *yet* is only used in that sense with Present or Past Perfect. *He hasn't gone back* would mean **by now**; but what the speaker meant was **by then**.

The Past Perfect can be a transfer to the pre-past of either the Present Perfect, as in [88] below or of the Past tense, as in [89]:

[88] The fax has arrived.
     – Yes, you told me it had (arrived).

[89] It came last night.
     – Yes, you told me it came (or had come) last night.

The Past Perfect is obligatory when it is a transfer of the Present Perfect [88]; and then it is not associated with an adverbial of past time. When it is a transfer of the Past, as in [89], the Past Perfect is optional (provided the meaning is clear without it), and a past time adverbial is allowable.

6   THE POST-PRESENT
7   THE FUTURE

It is impractical at this stage to separate our sixth and seventh aspects of time, so we begin by discussing them together.

While the past is a chronicle of facts, of events that can be reported objectively, the future is a tale untold, a mirage of events unfulfilled. At its most certain, the future is the sphere of things we expect to happen. We **expect**, i.e. we look out into the future and imagine something happening. The problems of future tense in English involve not only aspects of activity and time, but also moods, i.e. the certainty, hesitation, willingness, determination, hope, sense of obligation or of prohibition, or pure neutrality, with which the speaker views what is to come. The unreal world ahead of us is not defined nearly so sharply as the period before now. There is no clear division between post-present and future comparable to the clear distinction between pre-present and past. What may or may not happen in the future is referred to in a variety of ways. Each expression of futurity is often complicated by subjective attitudes on the part of the speaker and the audience; but that will be discussed further in the next chapter. At present, we are concerned with aspects of activity and of time.

As the future is referred to in a variety of ways, we shall find no one Future tense. But the following might be called examples of 'Future tenses':

1. Mr Turner will leave tomorrow. *(will)*

2. He is going to leave tomorrow. *(be + going to)*

3. He is leaving tomorrow. *(Present Continuous)*

4. He leaves tomorrow. *(Present Simple)*

5. He is to leave tomorrow. *(Be to)*

He is to leave tomorrow is typical of the English of journalism. In newspaper headlines, *is to leave* would be reduced to the infinitive, *to leave*. This can be a simple statement of fact, or of plans that will lead to fulfilment. *Be to* is also used as a modal, implying a command, as we shall see in the next chapter.

There is plenty of evidence for choosing *will* + infinitive as the most generally used expression of futurity in modern English. *Shall* may be regarded as an optional replacement for *will* in association with *I* and *we*. That statement is based on wide observation of actual educated usage; and it is made despite the old prescriptive rule, summarised thus:

	Singular	Plural
1st Person	I shall	we shall
2nd Person	you will	you will
3rd Person	he, she, it will	they will

That 'rule' has been taught so often, and insisted on so severely, that it has undoubtedly had its effect on 'careful' writing. Yet it is repeatedly broken, even by grammarians who teach it, as far as the use of *shall* is concerned. The prediction made by Kruisinga (in *A Handbook of Present-Day English* (1931-2)), that *shall* will ultimately disappear, has not yet come true, although *shan't* is rarely heard any more. As usage varies from region to region in the English-speaking world, and even from one individual speaker to another, there is no point in insisting on the prescriptive rule quoted above. In modern English *shall* with *I* and *we* is still common in offers and suggestions:

[90] Shall I pick you up at the station?

[91] Shall we have a break for a few minutes?

Shall is still used in positive sentences, but is relatively uncommon, and frequently we hear neither *I shall* nor *I will* but only *I'll*.

I O, I U, S O and **S U** can be applied to the *will* Future in exactly the same way as to the tenses we have discussed already. Thus:

[92] That's the phone. I'll answer it. **I O**

[93] Good-bye. I'll see you on Wednesday. **I O**

[94] Good-bye. I'll be thinking of you. **I U**

[95] I'll be thinking of you tomorrow. **I U**

[96] Don't worry. I'll write to you every day. **S O**

[97] I'll be working late every day next week. **S U**

Comparing examples [92] with [93], and [94] with [95], we can see that the Future with *will* can be used whether future time is specified or not. Contrast [92] with

[98] That's all right. I've answered it.

and [93] with

[99] Hello again. I saw you on Wednesday, didn't I?

Nevertheless, we **can** make a distinction between post-present, our sixth aspect of time, illustrated like this:

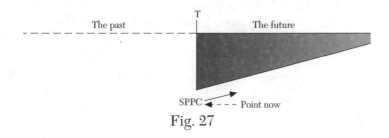

Fig. 27

and the future, detached from point now, our seventh aspect, illustrated thus:

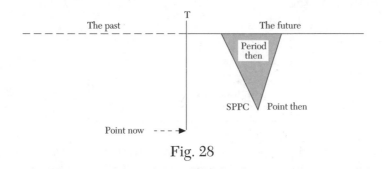

Fig. 28

We can make that distinction by using adverbials *from now on* or the more formal *henceforth* for the post-present, and *tomorrow, next Friday* etc. for the future. For example, compare example [92] with:

[100] Don't touch the phone again. I'll answer it from now on.

Note *I'll be thinking of you*. [94] and [95] are examples of **I U**, and [97] of **S U**. All three are examples of continuous aspect, [94] applied to the post-present, [95] and [97] applied to the future detached from now. However, the same construction, *will be + -ing*, can have two other uses:

[101] Mr Turner will be leaving on Thursday.

That may mean practically the same as *Mr T. is leaving on Thursday* or it may be intended as a plain statement of future fact. The 'plain statement' avoids any tone of command on the part of the speaker, or any suggestion of determination on the part of Mr Turner – a feeling that might be conveyed by the words *Mr Turner will leave on Thursday*. In fact, the use of the continuous in *will be leaving on Thursday* often suggests the avoidance of a too definite assertion as we saw in *I am hoping* etc. in 5.3.

Although the distinction between post-present and future is not so clear as that between pre-present and past, it is possible to trace a different kind of distinction between *will* + infinitive and the other 'future tenses' listed earlier. Suppose we adopt the symbol T, standing for 'time of utterance', and the symbol F, standing for 'future event'. Then I would say that, in *will* + infinitive, SPPC is at F, thus:

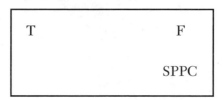

whereas with the other 'future tenses' SPPC is at T, with the speaker's attention directed towards F, thus:

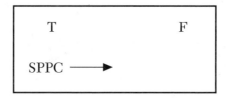

This means that in saying *Mr T. will leave tomorrow*, the speaker's primary concern is with the future event; whereas with *Mr T. is going to leave, is leaving, leaves* and *is to leave tomorrow*, the speaker's primary concern is with the **present** factors, arrangements, plans, intentions, or whatever, that are expected to lead to Mr T.'s departure. Thus in saying

[102] I'm going to call at the bank tomorrow and will pay the cheque in then.

my attention is first focused on T (my present intentions that will lead to F), then on F itself. However, the change from *I'm going to call* to *will pay* can also be accounted for (a) by an intuitive desire to avoid repeating the *-ing* form, and (b) by a shift from post-present to future, which is comparable with the shift from pre-present to past that we saw in [56] It is noticeable that a text making a series of predictions, such as a weather forecast, may begin with *going to* and then be restricted to *will*, as in the following example:

[103] Tomorrow is going to be colder everywhere. There will be snow on the hills; and motorists will find icy patches on many roads.

A choice between *will* and *be going to* often arises in ordinary spoken English: it is not likely to arise in formal written English, where *will* is usually preferred. When there is a choice, *be going to* is more appropriate when emphasis falls on present signs, intentions, preparations, etc., and *will* is more appropriate when such emphasis is absent or irrelevant. Note the presence or absence of the emphasis in the following examples:

[104] (The telephone rings.) All right, I'll answer it.

The situation does not require the emphasis. *I'm going to answer it* would suggest a sequence of consideration, decision, action and ultimate fulfilment, by the end of which the caller would have lost patience and rung off.

[105] I'm going to answer your letter, point by point.

Here the sequence of forethought, purpose, action and fulfilment is deliberately stressed.

[106] I'll answer it if you give me time.

The conditions which might lead to future action are not provided.

[107] I don't like this car. I'm going to sell it.

This breaks the news of my considered intentions and their possible consequence. Compare *I think I'll sell it*, where the idea of intention is absent; or *I'll sell it for 400 pounds*, where emphasis is on the price.

[108] Tomorrow is going to be a busy day. (So much has been planned, all the evidence points to it.)
    – Yes, it will be a busy day (emphasis not repeated).

[109] Tomorrow will be Tuesday.

Simple statement of future, with no justification for emphasis on T.

[110] I'm going to read your essay this evening and I'll discuss it with you tomorrow.

Emphasis on the first action, not repeated on the second.

[111] (I don't know the answer.) I'll know it next week.

In such a case, not only does emphasis fall on the point in future time, but the idea of purpose, action and fulfilment would be irrelevant with such an act of perception. It would not be irrelevant in *find out*, as in *I don't know the answer, but I'm going to find out.*

In temporal clauses (referring to time) and conditional clauses (beginning with *if, unless*, or a word of similar meaning), reference to the future is usually made in the Present tense, as in

[112] I'll come | when
         as soon as | I'm ready.

[113] We'll go out if it's fine.

There are two complications; first, we must distinguish between a temporal clause, referring to time, as in

[114] Tell me when you're ready.

and a noun clause, object of a verb, as in

[115] Tell me when you'll be ready.

Example [114] means: You will be ready at some future time. At that time, let me know. Example [115] means: Tell me now what that future time will be.

Second, an *if*-clause referring to the future may contain an implied prediction, foretelling the future, as in

[116] If you are alone next Saturday night, phone me.

The implied prediction in that sentence is: You will be alone on Saturday night. Note the tense in the if-clause of [116]. That example means: If the prediction comes true, phone me then. Compare that with

[117] If you will be alone on Saturday night, phone me.

That contains the same implied prediction: you will be alone on Saturday night. But [117] means: If that prediction can be safely made, telephone me now.

8 THE PRE-FUTURE: FUTURE PERFECT

The eighth aspect of time, the prelude to the future, expressed by the Future Perfect, is comparable with the Present and Past Perfects. It could be illustrated as follows:

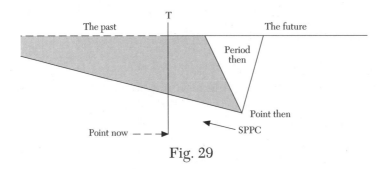

Fig. 29

The period which the speaker is now considering is imagined as being viewed from some future time, detached from now. The period may begin at any time before **Then** (future), either in the pre-future or before the present moment. In other words, the period may or may not have begun at the time of speaking:

[118] I haven't answered that letter yet, but I'll have done so by Friday. (On Friday I'll be able to look back and see that it has been answered.) (**I O**)

[119] I started writing this book six months ago. By the end of this week I'll have written 200 pages. (**I O**)

[120] By then, I'll have been writing it for just over six months. (**I U**)

[121] By the end of this year, the moon will have gone round the earth thirteen times. (**S O**)

In example [118], *I'll do so by Friday* would also be acceptable, but it does not give the emphasis explained in parenthesis. In [121], *will go* would be acceptable, but only if that statement is made early in January. In [119] and [120], where the pre-future period begins before the time of speaking, then *I'll have written* and *I'll have been writing* are essential to the sense.

Note that in the parenthesis in [118] I could have said *I'll be able to look back and see that it will have been answered*. But the use of the marked Future Perfect form, *will have been answered*, would make that sentence clumsy, so I used an unmarked form, *has been answered*, instead. Compare that with

[122] By the time I'm seventy, I shall have retired: and I'll get up late every morning when I've retired.

[123] I'll let you have this book on Friday, if I've finished by then.

In other words, in temporal and conditional clauses the Future Perfect is normally replaced by the Perfect, just as the Future was replaced by the Present in [112], and [113].

9 THE FUTURE AS SEEN FROM THE PAST: FUTURE-IN-THE-PAST

For this, the ninth aspect of time, the speaker's point of primary concern is in the past and the speaker's vision is directed forwards, to the more recent past, or to the present or even into the future:

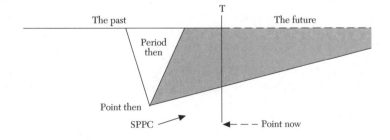

Fig. 30

This aspect of time occurs to the speaker when (s)he is reporting, from a viewpoint in the past, the kind of situation reflected in examples [92]-[97]:

[124] I said
| I'd answer it.
| I'd see you on Wednesday.
| I'd be thinking of you.
| etc.

Note the tenses used in the temporal and conditional clauses in:

[125] I said
| I'd come when I was ready. (See [112].)
| we'd go out if it was fine. ([113])
| we'd stay indoors until it stopped raining. ([114])
| I'd get up late when I'd retired.

The conversational *'d* in [124] and [125], before an infinitive (*come, see, be, go, stay, get*) would be replaced in formal written English by *would* or perhaps *should*. Before a past participle such as *retired* in [125], *'d* is a weak form for *had*.

Since the future seen from the past extends beyond point now, as in Fig. 30, it would not be illogical, nor contrary to widespread usage, to say

[126] I said
| I'll answer it.
| I'll see you on Wednesday.
| we'll (or we'd) be thinking of you tomorrow.

if the phone has not yet been answered, or if Wednesday or tomorrow have not yet come.

It is possible to express a continuation of the past comparable with the post-present. This is easily seen in

[127] What were we doing (**I U**, Past tense) last lesson?
You were telling us (**I U**, Past tense) about X, and then you were going to tell us (T ➤ F transferred to the past) about Y.

It is not so easily seen in

[128] George dropped in yesterday evening just for a chat. We were dining at the Jones's, but he simply wouldn't go, so we were terribly late.

There, *we were dining* is a past equivalent of *we are dining*, and means 'we had arranged to dine'. Similarly, *We sailed at three* is a past equivalent of Future No. 4 in

[129] We really couldn't lunch with you on our last day. We sailed at three and had so much to do before we left.

There, *We sailed at three* = We were due to sail then.

5.5 THE TENSES

The tenses are verbal forms and constructions which express aspects of activity combined with aspects of time. As examples, the tenses of the verb *ask*, in the active voice, are set out below, with the names that are now commonly attached to them:

Aspect of time	Aspect of activity	Example	Tense
1. Unlimited and	O	I ask	Simple Present
2. Present	U	I am asking	Present Continuous
3. Pre-present	O	I have asked	Present Perfect
	U	I have been asking	Present Perfect Continuous
4. Past	O	I asked	Simple Past
	U	I was asking	Past Continuous
5. Pre-past	O	I had asked	Past Perfect
	U	I had been asking	Past Perfect Continuous
6. Post-present and	O	I will ask	Simple Future
7. Future	U	I will be asking	Future Continuous
8. Pre-future		I will have asked	Future Perfect
		I will have been asking	Future Perfect Continuous
9. Future seen from the past	O	I would ask	Future-in-the-Past
	U	I would be asking	

Tenses in the passive voice would fit into a similar scheme:

1 and 2	I am asked
3	I have been asked
4	I was asked
5	I had been asked
6 and 7	I will be asked
8	I will have been asked
9	I would be asked

To the above, we must add *I used to ask, I used to be asked*, which can be regarded as a Past tense referring to habitual action no longer performed, and the other 'Future tenses' set out on page 77.

5.6 OTHER USES OF THE TENSES

The Simple Present is customarily used

(a) as the 'historic present' to make a narrative of past events seem more dramatic, and especially in a synopsis of a novel or play. Each new step in the story is related in the Simple Present, while the Present Continuous serves as a background against which action takes place:

[130] The villagers are quietly going about their daily tasks when a stranger rides up and startles them all by firing his pistol into the air.

(b) in newspaper headlines. Note that the detailed report beneath the headlines relates past events in the Past tense;

(c) in captions accompanying a picture illustrating past action, as in

[131] Aeneas carries his father out of burning Troy.

The Present Perfect Continuous, depending on the context in which it is used, can stress

(a) incompletion in contrast to completion:

[132] I've been reading your book (incompletion), and have already read the first three chapters (completion).

(b) a temporary state of affairs:

[133] We've been living in a hotel so far, but soon we hope to move into a furnished flat.

(c) irritation at somebody else's action:

[134] Who's been using my tape-recorder?

The Simple Past is used to refer to an act which is desirable or even obligatory but which has not yet been fulfilled:

[135] Hurry up! It's time we left.

It may also be used when the speaker is making a request or giving an invitation without assuming that the listener will agree:

[136] I wondered (meaning I wonder now) whether you could lend me your typewriter.

The Past Continuous may be used:

(a) to refer to past intentions, cancelled or otherwise unfulfilled. Whereas the dictator might declare *I cross the Rubicon tomorrow*, and the ordinary mortal say *I'm crossing it tomorrow*, an undecided person might reply thus:

[137] What are you doing tomorrow?
　　　– Well-er-I was crossing the Rubicon-but now-er.

i.e. I was thinking of crossing it before you asked me, but now I am willing to do whatever you suggest.

(b) similarly, in a hesitant request or invitation, as in [136]:

　　[138] I was wondering whether...

(c) to refer to action that ought to be in progress but has not yet started, as in [135]:

　　[139] Hurry up! It's time we were leaving.

Note once more how the continuous form is used to express a less definite attitude than the non-continuous form.

5.7 SEQUENCE OF TENSES

The question of which combination of tenses should be used in English in a piece of consecutive speech or writing is primarily a matter of deciding which tense is suitable for each separate action; and that, as we have seen earlier in this chapter, depends on the aspect of activity and the aspect of time with which the speaker is concerned, and on whether a marked or unmarked form is required. Take care of each tense, therefore, and the sequence will usually take care of itself. However, since sudden and too frequent changes of point of primary concern are undesirable unless deliberately intended, and can be confusing to the reader, Present tenses tend to be found with Present, Present Perfect and Future, while Past tenses tend to be found with Past, Past Perfect and Future-in-the-Past. In addition, there are four areas of particular difficulty as far as tense sequence is concerned. They are dealt with in the following paragraphs.

Firstly, for the tenses used in sentences with conditional and temporal clauses having future reference, look back at examples [112] – [117], and [122] – [123].

Secondly, for the tenses used in *if-* sentences generally, we must consider whether the *if-* clause assumes something to be a fact, or whether it imagines a non-fact to be actual fact. Thus:

Assuming a fact

(a) If you tell the truth, people trust you.

(b) If you are telling the truth, we have no time to lose.

(c) If you have studied all this book, you know a lot.

(d) If you have been walking in this heat, you must be very thirsty.

(e) If we told Father the truth, he never punished us.

(f) If you were walking all day yesterday, no wonder you are tired today.

(g) If you had met John before, why didn't you speak to him last night?

(h) If you had been swimming before breakfast yesterday, no wonder you ate such a lot.

(i) If you tell the truth tomorrow, you will be quite safe.

(j) If you are playing tennis next Saturday, we shall not be able to go for our usual walk.

(k) If you have read this report by next Friday, you will be able to discuss it at our meeting on Friday afternoon.

(l) Didn't I say that if you told the truth you would be quite safe?

Imagining non-fact to be actual fact

(m) (You never tell the truth.) If you told the truth, people would trust you.

(n) (You're not telling the truth.) If you were telling the truth, you would be looking me straight in the eye.

(o) (You have not told the truth.) If you had told the truth, you wouldn't have blushed like that.

(p) (You did not tell the truth.) If you had told the truth, you would not have been punished.

(q) (You had not met John before I introduced him to you.) If you had met him before, I am sure he would have recognised you.

(r) (We shall not go out in this rain.) If we went out, we should only get soaking wet.

(s) (We shall not be playing tennis tomorrow.) If we were playing tennis, we wouldn't be able to finish our work.

Thirdly, note the tenses used with *wish*, which also imagines non-fact to be actual fact:

(a) I'm not enjoying myself: I wish I was (or were).

(b) I'm working today: I wish I wasn't (or weren't).

(c) I can't swim: I wish I could.

(d) I don't feel well: I wish I felt better.

(e) I feel tired: I wish I didn't.

(f) I did not see that film: I wish I had seen it.

(g) I'll lend you my camera: I wish you would.

Finally, note the tenses commonly used in reporting speech in the past:

Direct speech	**Indirect speech**
(a) 'The shop's shut.'	He said the shop was shut.
(b) 'The men have gone.'	He said the men had gone.
(c) 'They went at 5 o'clock.'	He said they went (or had gone) at five o'clock.
(d) 'Someone will come.'	He said someone would come.
(e) 'I shall come.'	He said he would come.

Indirect speech can have the Past Perfect in both (b) and (c). However, while the Past Perfect is obligatory in (b), it is optional in (c). In (e), *shall* is optional with *I* or *we*, but only *will* or *would* occurs in plain future, or future-in-the-past, with *you* or *he*. *Can* and *may* in direct speech become *could* and *might* in indirect; but the *should* of obligation, and *must* and *ought to*, in direct speech remain unchanged when speech is reported as past. However, the changes of tenses in the dependent clause, though usual, are not obligatory if the reported fact is still valid, so that *He said the shop is shut*, *He said he will come* are quite acceptable if, when those statements are made, the shop still is shut, he still will come, and so on.

COMMENTARY AND DISCUSSION POINTS

In this chapter Close's nine aspects reveal the remarkable symmetry of the English verb, and reflect exactly the description outlined on page 28 of David Wilkins' *Notional Syllabuses*. In *The English Verb*, Michael Lewis provides the following diagram, which reflects nine similar aspects:

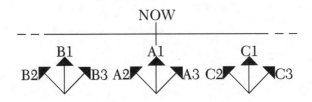

Lewis offers the following exemplifications of the nine forms shown on the diagram:

A.1.   I **swear** it wasn't me.
A.2.   **I've seen** him already.
A.3.   **I'm going to see** him tomorrow.

B.1.   I **saw** him yesterday
B.2.   **I'd seen** him before
B.3.   I **was going to see** him in the afternoon.

C.1.   **I'll see** him tomorrow
C.2.   **I'll have seen** him before Saturday
C.3.   **I'll be going to see** him when I get to London.

All of these analyses have one thing in common – they seek to show something about the **overall** structure of the verb, rather than simply dealing with individual points.

How does Close's analysis of the verb in this chapter contrast with the way it is frequently done in the textbooks or student grammars? What advantages can you see to having an over-view? Can you see any advantage to students having an over-view, or do you believe it is best for them to learn by studying particular uses one by one?

What role do you think diagrams can play in helping you, or your students, to understand the underlying meaning of verb forms? Do you find diagrams helpful?

6 Auxiliary and Modal Verbs

6.1 INTRODUCTION

<table>
<tr><td colspan="2" align="center">Auxiliaries</td><td colspan="2" align="center">Modals</td></tr>
<tr><td align="center">A</td><td align="center">B</td><td align="center">C</td><td align="center">D</td></tr>
<tr><td>(a) am('m)</td><td>—</td><td>(f) will('ll)</td><td>won't</td></tr>
<tr><td>is('s)</td><td>isn't</td><td>shall</td><td>shan't</td></tr>
<tr><td>are('re)</td><td>aren't</td><td>would('d)</td><td>wouldn't</td></tr>
<tr><td>was</td><td>wasn't</td><td>should</td><td>shouldn't</td></tr>
<tr><td>were</td><td>weren't</td><td></td><td></td></tr>
<tr><td></td><td></td><td>(g) can</td><td>can't</td></tr>
<tr><td>(b) have('ve)</td><td>haven't</td><td>could</td><td>couldn't</td></tr>
<tr><td>has('s)</td><td>hasn't</td><td>may</td><td>—</td></tr>
<tr><td>had('d)</td><td>hadn't</td><td>might</td><td>mightn't</td></tr>
<tr><td></td><td></td><td>must</td><td>mustn't</td></tr>
<tr><td></td><td></td><td>ought</td><td>oughtn't</td></tr>
<tr><td>(c) do</td><td>don't</td><td></td><td></td></tr>
<tr><td>does</td><td>doesn't</td><td>(h) need</td><td>needn't</td></tr>
<tr><td>did</td><td>didn't</td><td>dare</td><td>daren't</td></tr>
<tr><td>(d) will('ll)</td><td>won't</td><td></td><td></td></tr>
<tr><td>shall</td><td>shan't</td><td></td><td></td></tr>
<tr><td>would('d)</td><td>wouldn't</td><td></td><td></td></tr>
<tr><td>should</td><td>shouldn't</td><td></td><td></td></tr>
<tr><td>(e) used</td><td>use(d)n't</td><td></td><td></td></tr>
</table>

What are here called auxiliaries include:

(a) parts of the verb *be* which are used with *-ing* to form the continuous (*I am working*) or with *-ed* to form the passive (*I am asked*)

(b) parts of the verb *have* used to form the perfective (*have worked, have been working, had worked* etc)

(c) parts of the verb *do*, used to form the interrogative and the negative of the Simple Present and the Simple Past

(d) *will* and *shall* which, with the bare infinitive, form the principal Future; and *would* and *should* which form a Future-in-the-Past, at least in indirect speech form

(e) *used* + *to*-infinitive referring to a past state of affairs no longer prevailing

What are here called the modals include:

(f) *will, shall, would* and *should*

(g) *can, could, may, might, must* and *ought*

(h) *need* and *dare,* which may be used as modals or as 'full verbs'.

The functions of the modals will be the main theme of this chapter.

6.2 OPERATORS

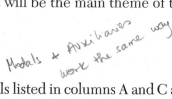

Modals & Auxiliaries work the same way.

The auxiliaries and the modals listed in columns A and C above have one important syntactic feature in common: they act as 'operators' in the following six operations:

1. Followed immediately by *not*, they make the verbal part of a sentence negative, as in

[1] We have not finished breakfast yet.

The reduced forms are usual in fluent, unemphasised, everyday speech. Thus *we have* or *we have not* before *finished* would be typical of formal writing and deliberate speech; *we've, we've not* or *we haven't* before *finished* would be typical of normal speech and informal writing. Note that in Columns B and D, operator + *n't* is written as one word.

2. Operator + subject + rest of the verb provides the interrogative form:

[2] Have you finished breakfast yet?

3. Operator + *n't* + subject + rest of the verb provides the negative-interrogative form:

[3] Haven't you finished breakfast yet?

Have you not finished? would be either more formal or more deliberate. More formal still would be a construction like *Have not instructions been published?* (which is unusual when the subject is a personal pronoun).

4. The operators supply the verbal part of tag questions:

[4] You've finished, haven't you?
     You haven't finished, have you?

The operator and its tense in the tag must be the same as those in the main part of the sentence.

[margin, handwritten, rotated] Have you not slept? / Have you not slept?

5. The operators supply an emphatic affirmative, as in

[5]   I interrupted you. You haven't finished.
   – That's all right. I have finished. (*have* stressed)

6. They act as a substitute for the whole of the predicate, avoiding repetition, as in

[6]   George hasn't finished breakfast, but we have.

In the active voice, the Simple Present and the Simple Past contain no operator; and *do, does, did* supply this lack for the six operations just listed. The main verb is then in the bare infinitive (without *to*) whatever the subject and tense may be. Thus:

1. [7]   He likes coffee but he doesn't like tea.

2. [8]   Does he take sugar? Did he always take it?

3. [9]   Don't you like it? Doesn't he? Didn't he like it?

4. [10] You like milk, don't you?
         You didn't always like it, did you?

5. [11] You don't like cream, do you?
         – Oh, but I do like it. (*do* stressed)

6. [12] I think you made the right choice. In fact, we all do.

Do is also used to form the negative-imperative (e.g. *Do not speak to the driver. Don't move*) as well as an emphatic form of the imperative (*Do be quiet*).

Some restrictions or exceptions

All the auxiliaries and modals can be used in those six ways, except at the following points:

(a) The reduced forms in columns A and C (*'m*, *'ll*, etc.) will not occur at the very beginning or very end of a sentence or clause. Thus:

[13] I think it's beginning to snow?
     – Is it? Why, so it is.

(b) There is no alternative negative form to *I'm not*; but *Aren't I?* can informally replace *Am I not?*

(c) *Used*, which requires the *to*-infinitive, fits easily into operation 5; but in the other cases there is popular pressure against such forms as *Use(d) n't you to (do that)?*, as well as uncertainty about how *use(d) n't* should be spelt. On the other hand, the widely heard *didn't use(d) to, Did you use(d) to?*

Didn't you use(d) to? have not gained complete respectability. The following would, I consider, be acceptable ways of overcoming these difficulties:

1. Now I type my letters but I used not to. (or usedn't to)

2. & 3. Did(n't) you (usually) type them?

4. You used to type them, didn't you?

5. I don't type my letters now, but I used to. (*used* stressed).

6. I used to write everything by hand, and so did my brother.

(d) *Ought*, also followed by the *to*-infinitive, presents similar problems. There is some popular reluctance to say *ought not to*, but *didn't ought to* is generally regarded as sub-standard. Any uncertainty about using *ought* can usually be overcome by replacing it by *should*. The following would therefore be acceptable:

1. You ought not to (or oughtn't to) say that.

2. What ought we to do now?

3. Oughtn't we to leave? Or more formal Ought we not to?

4. We ought to go now, oughtn't (or shouldn't) we?

5. I haven't read that book, but I know I ought to. (*ought* stressed)

6. Yes, you ought to read it, and so should I.

(e) *Cannot* is normally spelt as one word. But there is a difference between *You cannot stay here*, where *can* is negated, and *You can not stay if you prefer to leave*, where *stay* is negated. A similar comment would apply to the other modals. *You could not* (or *couldn't*) *stay* negates *could*, whereas *You could not stay* (*not* stressed, and separated from *could*) negates *stay*.

(f) *Mayn't* is excluded as old-fashioned and now very rarely heard. (Incidentally *shan't* is now also rare and seems to be disappearing.)

(g) *Need* and *dare* only occur as modals before a bare infinitive and with negative or interrogative meanings. As 'full verbs', they could be used in all the six operations with the help of *do*:

Modal	**Full verb**
1. I need/dare not go.	You don't need/dare to go.
2. Need/Dare we go?	Do we need/dare to go?
3. —	Don't you need/dare to go?

4. We needn't/daren't go yet,   We don't need/dare to go yet, do we?
   need/dare we?

5.   —   You say I don't need/dare to go, but I do.
                                 (*do* stressed)

6.   —   John needs to read this again and so do I.

In the Modal column, 3 is unfilled since *Needn't we go?* implies an affirmative. On the other hand, *I hardly/scarcely need tell you* would be acceptable, as semi-negatives.

6.3 THE MODALS – GENERAL

Will can be a purely temporary auxiliary, foretelling the future. At the same time, it can be a modal expressing some personal attitude towards an unfulfilled event. *Will/shall* + infinitive therefore belong both to a time system and to a modal system, thus:

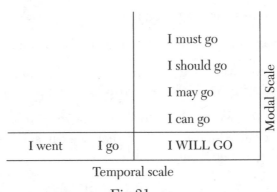

Fig 31

All the modals, except *shall*, have two main functions, which we may call primary and secondary. In their primary function, they express some degree of freedom, or lack of freedom, to act—from complete liberty to inescapable prohibition; and this freedom, or lack of it, can apply to the speaker, or to the person(s) being addressed, or to some person(s) to whom the speaker is referring.

In their secondary function, all except *shall* act as one of the devices English has for allowing the speaker to give a personal evaluation of the truth of the statement the speaker is making. Other devices include the use of *seem* and verbs of similar meaning, as in *It seems to be raining over there*, and 'disjunct' adverbials (see page 152), as in *Apparently, we had a lot of rain last night*. We shall see the difference between these two functions as we examine each of the modals in turn.

6.4 WILL

In its primary function, *will* can express certainty, or volition, or a combination of both certainty that nothing can stop the event from taking place, or the will to ensure that it is accomplished. The speaker's own certainty and/or volition could be an important feature in

[14] We will find a cure for cancer.

[15] He will do what I tell him.

and

[16] Let our motto be: I will not be afraid.

The will of the person addressed is referred to in

[17] May I help you?
  – Yes, if you will.

A third person's volition is suggested in

[18] Mr Turner will see you soon. He won't keep you long.

[19] Some people will leave this door open. (*will* strongly stressed and indicating persistent habit). They **won't** close it properly.

[20] That old man will sit there for hours looking out to sea.
  (He has done it so often before that one can safely predict that it will happen again and again.)

How much volition is expressed by *will* depends on many factors, including the speaker's own intentions, the context of the utterance, the animateness or inanimateness of the subject, the degree to which the action is subject to human control. There is no volition, but there may be certainty, in *The rain will come soon*; there may be volition as well as certainty in *Mr Turner will come soon*. There may be no volition in *We'll know the results tomorrow*, but plenty of it in *We'll find out the results now*.

The modal *will* is commonly used in questions:

[21] Will you have some tea? (What are your wishes?)

[22] Won't you have some more? (What are your wishes?)

[23] Will you post this letter for me? (Those are my wishes:
  I hope you are willing to carry them out.)

[24] Will you sit down! (That is my wish and command.)

Note that [21], [22] and [23] would be spoken with a rising intonation, but [24] with a sharply falling one.

There is no restriction on the use of the modal *will* in *if*-clauses, thus:

[25] If you will smoke, please go outside.

[26] If you will sit down for a moment I will see if Mr Turner is in.

In its secondary function, *will* allows the speaker to make a statement, not asserting that it is true but suggesting that it will prove to be so. *I suppose* or *I expect* can usually, and often is, added to the statement:

[27] (The phone rings.) That will be Jeremy, I expect.

[28] I wonder where the boys are. They'll be coming home from school now, I suppose.

Will Have-ed

Besides expressing the Future Perfect, *will have-ed* can indicate a present supposition about the pre-present or past, as in

[29] You will all have heard the news last night.

That means *I suppose that you heard*. . . . Without the adverbial of past time, *last night*, it could also mean *I suppose that you have heard*....

6.5 WOULD

Would has a temporal function, and serves as a Future-in-the-Past, in past reported speech (*I told you it would rain*.). It rarely serves this purpose in an independent clause, though it can do so in the course of a narrative, as in

[30] The climbers had reached 5,000 metres. Soon they would see the summit.

In conditional sentences, whereas the Present tense in the *if*-clause commonly accompanies *will* in the main clause, the Past tense in the *if*-clause attracts *would* in the main:

[31] If you heated this liquid, it would explode.

That is an example of what is called the Conditional *would*.

Would can also act as the past equivalent of the modal *will* in past reported speech. Thus example [14] could become:

[14a]   I told you we would find a cure.......

and a similar comment would apply to examples [15]–[24] inclusive. Thus:

> [23a]　I asked you if you would post this letter.

Exercises requiring students to 'put *will* into the past tense' are often meaningless (unless past reported speech is intended). *Will you have some tea?* is an utterance that only makes sense if it applies to present time, and it is not made past by converting *Will* into *Would*! A similar remark applies to all the examples [14]–[18] inclusive, and to [21]–[24] inclusive. However, [19] and [20] can be 'put into the past tense', in the following way:

> [19a]　Some people would leave this door open. They wouldn't close it properly. So now we keep it locked.

> [20a]　The old man would sit there for hours.

Example [20a] is typical of narrative style.

Would you have some tea? is an illustration of *would* as a separate modal, expressing meanings that are similar to those of the modal *will*, but more hesitantly, and with greater deference to the audience. The same applies to examples [22]-[24], where the speaker also has a choice between *will* and *would*. But *will* could not replace *would* in these examples:

> [32] Would you like some tea, or would you prefer coffee?

> [33] Would you mind posting this letter for me?

The modal *would* occurs freely in *if*-clauses. Thus:

> [34] If you would take a seat for a moment, I'll see if Mr Turner is in.

Would there suggests willingness on your part. It makes a hesitant suggestion in:

> [35] If you would be interested, I'll send you a copy.

A special idiomatic use of *would* is found in an example indicating characteristic behaviour such as:

> [36] I've lost my ticket.
> 　　 – You would. (*would* stressed)

Would or Should?

Should can, optionally, replace *would* with *I* and *we* in the Future-in-the-Past and Conditional uses. But this replacement could cause ambiguity: *should* in *I told you we should find a cure* .. might be mistaken for the *should* of obligation.

Note:

[37] I should be grateful if you would reply urgently.

which takes advantage of the option of using *should* with *I* or *we* and avoids the repetition of *would*. Replacement of *would* by *should* is unacceptable when *would* is a modal in its own right, as in

[38] I was never good at football. I would miss the ball completely.

[39] I would willingly help you, if I were free.

Would has a secondary modal function, allowing the speaker to make a statement but with less certainty than in the corresponding sentences with *will*:

[27a]   (The phone rings.) That would be Jeremy, probably.

[28a]   The boys would be coming home from school, I imagine.

Would Have-ed

Would have-ed can be a transfer of the Future Perfect to the past, so that *I'll have finished that by Friday* can become *I told you I'd have finished....*

It can be a transfer of the Conditional *would* to the past, so that *If I met him again, I would recognise* him can become *If I had met him again, I would have recognised him.*

It can also be a present, hesitant assumption about past action, *would* serving the secondary modal function, as in

[27a]   Someone telephoned you last night.
        – That would have been Jeremy, I would say.

6.6 SHALL   *Americans don't really use Shall, unless they want to sound fancy or cute. "Shall we?"*

Shall, like *will* can be a purely temporary auxiliary, optionally replacing *will* with *I* and *we*. Even in its temporal use, however, there may be a private colouring. Personally, I use *will* as a weak unmarked form, a neutral indicator of the future, or as a strong unmarked form combining prediction with certainty; and I use *shall* as a marked form, expressing modesty (I hope) towards my audience and readers. This already suggests that I use *shall* as a modal, in the sense of 6.3. I realise that, with other speakers and writers, the decision to use *shall* instead of *will* with *I* or *we* may be a matter of taste, habit or chance.

Shall is certainly a modal, expressing the speaker's deference to the wishes of the audience, in:

[40] Shall I open the window? (i.e. would you like me to do that?)

[41] Shall we go, or do you want to stay longer?

[42] Shall we have coffee now?

Shall, as a modal is also a mark of decision or determination on the part of the speaker(s) with regard to the actions of others, as in

[43] There shall be no more wars.

— a wise decree, deciding that everyone must henceforth live in peace, but not an assurance that war will never occur again.

[44] The enemy shall not pass. (We are determined not to let them.)

[45] Every member shall pay the annual subscription within the first fortnight of the year.

— a decision affecting every member of a certain organisation, but not an assurance that every member will pay promptly.

[46] You shall have whatever you want, I promise you.

Shall Have-ed

Shall have-ed expresses Future Perfect and is available, optionally, with *I* and *we*.

6.7 SHOULD

(a) *I shall be late* can become *I told you I should be late* in indirect speech.

(b) Also in indirect speech, examples [40]-[42] would become *I asked if I should open...* etc. [44] would become *We were determined the enemy should not pass*; and [46], *I promised you should have whatever you wanted*.

In its primary function, the modal *should* suggests an obligation (that is escapable) or action that is advisable:

[47] Applications should be submitted by March 31st at the latest. (Quotation from an official document.)

[48] You should take more exercise. (That is advisable.)

[49] I should take more exercise, if I were you.

In [49] the speaker tactfully lays the obligation on himself, though it is intended for the person addressed.

'Suggestive' or 'putative' should

Should also makes a supposition. In

[50] If you should be interested, I'll send you a copy,

the speaker is more hesitant in supposing that you are interested than in example [35] and still more hesitant in

[51] Should you be interested (by any chance)....

where *should* is usually strongly stressed and is not replaceable by *would*.

The 'suggestive' or 'putative' use of *should* also occurs in

[52] I'm surprised that you should feel so upset.

Should could be omitted from [52], in which case my surprise would have been caused by the **fact** that you are upset. The use of *should* in [52] suggests that I am surprised by the **idea** of your being upset now. In:

[53] It is right that we should tell him the truth,

should, referring to future action, cannot be omitted. Notice the difference between

[54] I propose that Mr Turner should be Chairman.

where *should* could be omitted, leaving *be* as a subjunctive, and

[55] I believe that he should be Chairman.

where *should* cannot be left out. [54] makes a proposal about the future, while [55] only states what course of action somebody considers desirable. *Should* remains unchanged if [54] and [55] are reported in the past, e.g.

[56] I proposed/believed that he should be Chairman.

Note the special use of *should* in:

[57] I can't understand why you should say that. (i.e. I can't understand that makes you say it now)

In its secondary function, *should* is a device by which the speaker can indicate that (s)he supposes the statement (s)he is making to be true :

[58] According to the map, this should be our way.

Should Have-ed

Should have-ed can

(a) optionally replace *would have-ed* with *I* and *we*

(b) refer to past obligation unfulfilled. Compare example [47] with

> [59] Your application is too late. You should have submitted it by March 31st.

Similarly, *should not have-ed* refers to action taken in the past despite obligation not to take it, as in *You should not have left it till it was too late.*

(c) *Should have-ed* refers to the past in

> [52a] I'm surprised that you should have felt upset. (i.e. I'm surprised at the idea of your being upset then)

> [57a] I can't understand why you should have said that. (I can't understand what made you say it).

(d) As with the other modals, in the secondary function *should have-ed* marks a present supposition about the past:

> [58a] We took the wrong road an hour ago. According to the map, the road going east should have been our way.

6.8 OUGHT

Ought to and *should* are often inter-replaceable, but only in the sense of obligation. Thus [48] could be re-worded:

> [48a] You ought to take more exercise.

But *ought to* would not be acceptable instead of *should* in [49]. To some speakers, *ought to* suggests an obligation the fulfilment of which is overdue or may be delayed. In the official statement in [47], if *should* were replaced by *ought to*, readers might suppose that it would not matter if applications were submitted after the date mentioned. A clerk receiving an enquiry about applications on, say, March 30th, could rightly say

> [59a] You'll have to make up your mind quickly. Applications ought to be in by tomorrow, and I doubt whether yours will arrive in time.

Ought to could not replace *should,* in any of the other examples in 6.7 except [55], which was only included in that paragraph as a contrast with [54].

In its secondary function, *ought to* has a meaning equivalent to that of *should* in its secondary function, exemplified by [58].

Ought to Have-ed

(a) *Ought to have-ed* refers to past obligation unfulfilled, and could replace *should have-ed* in example [59]. Similarly, *ought not to have-ed* refers to action taken despite obligation not to take it.

(b) In the secondary function, *ought to have-ed* could replace *should have-ed*, as in [58a].

6.9 MUST, HAVE TO, BE TO

Must differs from *should* and *ought to* in that it indicates obligation that is considered inescapable: *We must be free, or die* as Wordsworth put it.

The past equivalent of *must* is *had to*, though *must* can remain in past reported speech:

[60] 'I must be very frank with you.'

refers to the present, while

[60a]   I had to be very frank with him.

refers to the past. [60] could also refer to the future, though *I'll have to be very frank* makes the future reference clearer. [60] in past reported speech could either be *I told him I must be very frank...* or *I told him I had to be....* The latter would make it clear that the obligation belonged to the past.

There are two ways of negating *must* + infinitive: we can express an absence of obligation, by saying, e.g. *You need not go*, or *You do not have to go*; or we can negate what follows *must*, and say, for example, *You must not go*: Thus:

You need not go = You are **not required** to go.

You must not go = You are **required not** to go.

Have to (do something), or, informally, *have got to* (do it) suggests that the obligation is prescribed by some authority, regulation, or by unavoidable circumstances. *Have to* is not included as a modal as defined earlier, since *have* in this construction can be used as a full verb, with the complete range of inflections and tenses.

I am to (do something) means that I am obliged to do it by a plan, agreement, timetable or instruction, or something similar, which I am not free to ignore. Note the journalistic

[61] Henderson is to stay as Finance Minister.

which simply makes a statement about the future, a statement based on known plans, while

[61a]   You are to stay here. You are not to leave this room.

are firm commands.

The following table shows how the idea of obligation without the option of avoiding it is expressed in the various tenses, and how *have to* fulfils some functions which cannot be expressed with *must*:

Tense	Affirmative		Opposite	Negative
Present	(i)	I am obliged to go	am forbidden to	am not obliged to
	(ii)	I must (go)	must not	need not
	(iii)	I have to (go)	— (1)	do not have to
	(iv)	I am to(go)	am not to	—
Pre-Present	(i)	I have been obliged to	have been forbidden to	have not been obliged to
	(ii)	—	—	—
	(iii)	have had to	—	have not had to
Past	(i)	I was obliged to	was forbidden to	was not obliged to
	(ii)	must	must not	did not need to
	(iii)	had to	—	did not have to
	(iv)	was to(2)	was not to	—
Pre-Past	(i)	had been obliged to	had been forbidden to	had not been obliged to
	(ii)	—	—	—
	(iii)	had had to	—	had not had to
	(iv)	was to have (gone)(3)	—	—
Future	(i)	will be obliged to	will be forbidden to	will not be obliged to
	(ii)	must	must not	need not/will not need to
	(iii)	will have to	—	will not have to
	(iv)	am to	am not to	—

Notes 1. A blank in the table indicates that the corresponding form is not used in that position. 2. *I was to go to London*=that was the plan, those were my instructions. 3. *I was to have gone*= It had been planned that I should go, but I had not gone.

In its secondary function, *must* suggests that the truth of the speaker's statement is inescapable:

[62] This must be the way, surely.

The speaker feels no doubt about it. Note that the contrary to [62] would be:

[63] This can't be the way, surely.

Must Have-ed

This construction is used only in the secondary function of *must,* so that

[64] You must have been tired. (= I'm sure you were tired.)

[65] You can't have gone to the right house. (= I'm sure you did not...)

6.10 CAN

You can go means that you have complete freedom to act, whether that freedom depends on (a) your own ability; (b) lack of opposition; (c) positive permission; or (d) what circumstances allow.

[66] You can drive my car. < *ability (present)*
permission (present or future)

may refer to your present ability or to the permission given to you by the speaker. But

[67] You can drive my car perfectly, – *ability*

refers only to your ability. Example [66] could refer to future (as well as present) but only with the meaning of permission, not ability. To express future ability, one would have to say e.g.

[68] You'll be able to drive it perfectly after a few more lessons.

However, in an *if*-clause we can use can to refer to future ability:

[69] If you can use this typewriter properly in a month's time, you may keep it.

Freedom from other engagements is suggested in:

[70] I can see you tomorrow, at 10 o'clock.

though *I'll be able to see you* marks the future reference more strongly.

Can frequently precedes verbs of perception, e.g. *I can see a ship. Can you hear me? I can remember exactly what happened.* In such examples, the meaning is almost identical with that of *I see. Do you hear? I remember.* However, in *I can see* etc. we are more concerned with the freedom to perceive, rather than with the result. This appears clearly in the past: *We had a marvellous view from the top—we could see for miles*; but *Have you seen my watch anywhere? Yes, I saw it on your dressing-table.*

Can, in a question, can ask permission, as in

[71] Can I borrow your pen, please?

To that, the answer could be *Yes of course you can* (permission granted, as in one interpretation of example [66]), or *No, I'm afraid you can't.*

In its secondary function, *can* suggests that it is perfectly possible that the statement the speaker is making is true:

[72] This can be the answer, I think.

In this sense, *can* often begins a question, as in *Can this be right?*

Can Have-ed

An example of the secondary function of *can,* making a present assumption about the past or pre-past, would be

[73] He can have been delayed. (= I think it is possible he was, or has been, delayed.)

6.11 COULD

(a) *Can* becomes *could* when in past reported speech:

[66a] You said I could drive your car.

[71a] I asked if I could borrow your pen.

(b) *Could* refers to past ability, as in

[74] I could drive perfectly ten years ago.

We can interpret [74] as meaning not only that I had the ability but also that I succeeded in driving perfectly on many occasions. *We could see Mont Blanc* clearly implies that we actually saw it. But when we are referring to a single accomplishment subject to human control, *could* refers only to ability, not to the accomplishment itself. Thus:

[75] I could pass my driving test.

does not mean that I actually passed it. Accomplishment in that case could be expressed by *I was able*, or *I managed to pass it* or *I succeeded in passing it* or, simply, *I passed it*. On the other hand, *I could not pass my test* means that I lacked the ability, and therefore failed.

(a) *Could* refers to possible freedom from other engagements in:

[70a] I could see you tomorrow at 10, perhaps.

which is less definite than *I can see you...* .

(b) *Could* also asks for, and grants, permission, as in

[71b] Could I borrow your pen, please?

to which the answer might be *Yes of course you could* or *No I'm afraid you couldn't*. There, *could* is more hesitant, less direct, than *can*.

In its secondary function, *could* serves a similar purpose to that of *can*, but suggests some doubt as well as possibility. Thus:

[76] This could be the answer. What do you think?

Like *can* in this sense, *could* often begins a question: *Could this be right?*

Could Have-ed

This expresses past ability unused, or past permission of which advantage was not, or has not been, taken:

[77]   Did you get to the top (of the mountain)?
       – We could have done, but we didn't try.

[78]   Why did you walk? You could have taken my car. I said you could use it.

[76a] That could have been the answer. (= I assume now that that answer was probably right, though I am still doubtful about it.)

Note the example:

[79] When I saw the results I could have wept.(= I felt like weeping, but did not.)

6.12 BE ABLE TO

Just as *have to* is strongly associated with *must*, so *be able to* and *be unable to* are associated with *can*. Thus to express the idea of *can* in the infinitive, present participle, and present perfect, we can say:

[80] Candidates must be able to speak English fluently.

[81] Being able to speak both languages, you must act as interpreter.

[82] We have been unable to trace your reply to our letter of 17th November.

We are unable to is often preferred in formal English to the more abrupt *cannot* and the still more abrupt *can't*.

6.13 MAY

May can replace *can* in

[66] You can drive my car.

but then refers only to permission.

Similarly, *may* can replace *can* in example [71]:

[71c] May I borrow your pen, please?

May would there sound more hesitant than *can* and, to some people, more polite. A normal answer to *May I...* would be *Yes, of course you may* or *No you may not*, though one would not be surprised by the reply *Of course you can*.

In *can v may*, *can* might be considered as an unmarked form, frequently used in everyday conversation, while *may* is often a marked form deliberately used to stress the fact that permission is being sought and granted.

In the secondary function, *may* is very often used. Whereas *can* in [72] refers to one possibility that is open, *may* suggests that there are two or more possibilities, both or all of which are worth considering. Thus:

[83] This *may* be the answer. (*may* stressed)

suggests that the answer referred to is possibly the right one but that there are other possible answers. In [83], *may* refers to the present. It refers to future in

[84] I may be late home this evening. (= Perhaps I will, perhaps not.)

In this sense, *may not* is also often used. But the interrogative is best avoided. *Might this be the answer?* would be a normal interrogative transformation for [83]; while *May I be late this evening?* asks for permission to come home late, as in [71c]. An acceptable question related to [84] would be:

[84a]   Will you (or Are you likely to) be late this evening?

May Have-ed

Here again, the speaker makes a present assumption about the pre-present or the past. Thus:

[85] He's late (or He was late). He may have been delayed by fog.

means 'I think one of the possible explanations of his lateness is that he has been delayed by fog.'

6.14 MIGHT

Might is only the Past tense of *may* in indirect speech, as in

[66a]   You said I might drive your car.

[84a]   He said he might be home late.

In direct speech, *You might drive my car* is not a translation of *You may drive* . . . into the past: the past equivalent of *You may drive it* would be *You could have driven it* (see [78]).

Might expresses the maximum degree of hesitancy in requests for permission:

[71c]   Might I borrow your pen, please?

A polite answer to that request would be *Certainly.* Vague possibility, rather than positive permission, would be suggested by *Yes, you might,* while *No you might not* would be an abrupt refusal.

In the secondary function, *might* expresses the minimum degree of certainty in an assumption, as in *That might be the answer but I doubt it.* In *You know what the answer is: you might tell me* (stressed *tell*), the speaker is suggesting that the person addressed **should** give the answer.

Might Have-ed

Here the speaker is very hesitantly making a present assumption about the pre-present or the past:

[85a]   I can't imagine why he is (or was) late.
        – Nor can I. He might have been delayed by fog, or he might have
        had an accident.

In [85a], perhaps there was an accident, perhaps not. In:

[85b]   He might have been killed.

perhaps he was killed, perhaps not. But in:

[86] You were lucky. You might have been killed.

obviously the person addressed is not dead, but the chances of his being killed were considerable. In

[87] You knew the answer. You might have told me.

the speaker is expressing regret at not having been told sooner.

[88] It was terribly cold in that house. I might have been in the Arctic.

does not mean that the speaker had been in the Arctic but that the temperature in the house seemed as low as it would have been in the Arctic Circle. Finally, when we say:

[89] Life is full of might-have-beens.

we mean that many things in life could or should have happened but have not actually taken place.

6.15 MIGHT/MAY AS WELL; HAD BETTER; WOULD RATHER/SOONER

These modal-type expressions frequently occur in everyday conversation. *Might/May as well* suggests, or agrees to, a course of action, as in

[90] Here comes a bus. We might as well take it.
  – Yes, we might as well.

It can also suggest that a different course of action would be preferable:

[91] How slow this bus is! We might as well walk.
  – Yes, we might as well have gone on walking.

This construction does not occur in the interrogative or negative, but the verb following it can be negated:

[92] It's impossible to bring our car into town these days.
  – No, we might (just) as well not have one.

However, *it might be as well to* can have an interrogative form, e.g. *Might(n't) it* (or more formally *Might it not*) *be as well to consult a lawyer?*

Had better suggests a course of action that seems advisable; *would rather/sooner* a course that the speaker prefers:

[93] You've done enough. I think you'd better stop.
  – No, I'd rather go on a little longer.

The verb following *had better* and *would rather* can be negated, e.g. *You'd better not stop. I'd rather not go on*. Other possible transformations are: *Hadn't we better ask? Would* (or *Wouldn't*) *you rather let me drive*? But the full range of normal negative, interrogative and negative-interrogative transformations does not apply to the constructions in these two paragraphs.

6.16 NEED AND DARE

Need is used as a modal verb to express an attitude toward unfulfilled activity or as a 'full verb', as in

[94] Do you need this piece of paper? Someone needs/needed it.

There may be a distinction between *We need not stay*, i .e. we are not obliged to and *We don't need to stay*, meaning 'It isn't necessary for us to stay.' Note also that *You needn't have done that* suggests that you have done something unnecessarily, while *You didn't need to do it* means that, whether you have done it or not, there was no obligation or necessity for the action. Thus, if I am invited to a party and take my hostess a large bunch of flowers, she might say either

[95] Oh, you didn't need to do that,

in which case SPPC is at the point in past time when I bought the flowers, or

[96] Oh, you needn't have done that

in which case SPPC is at Point Now.

Dare is likewise both a modal and an ordinary, non-modal verb followed by the infinitive, with or without *to*. In its modal form, *daren't* can be used for present and past, thus:

Present I daren't look down *or* I don't dare (to).....
Past   I daren't look down *or* I didn't dare (to).....

The negative is carried over from the main clause to the subordinate in *I'm not sure that I dare go in*. The modal *dare* occurs exceptionally in the affirmative in *I dare say you're right*.

COMMENTARY AND DISCUSSION POINTS

As Close points out, the auxiliaries provide an extraordinarily regular feature of English. The use of part of the verb (*do*) – *do does did* – as a 'dummy auxiliary' maintains the patterns discussed in 6.2. As this paragraph clearly shows, and contrary to much presentation in language teaching text books, the English verb system is a great deal more regular than is often thought.

Do the operator patterns of 6.2. suggest alternative, and perhaps better ways of teaching? Is a different order of presentation suggested? What do you think is the best way to introduce the use of (*do*) as an operator to classes – as an 'exception' or as part of the general pattern of the verb?

Most modern course books tend to present the modal auxiliaries in functional expressions, rather than as purely structural items. Do you see advantages in this? Do you see any advantage in gathering the modals together as a group for teaching purposes?

In chapter 5 Close drew attention to the regular, symmetric nature of the verb. This is apparent again in this chapter if you look again at the sub-sections which indicate modal + perfect *have-ed.*

7   Verb and Adjective Patterns

Although the basic information in this chapter belongs to the 'solid core' of English grammatical facts (see p4), it is included as an essential preliminary to the chapters on the infinitive and the -*ing* form, and on the section of phrasal verbs in Chapter 9.

Every English sentence and clause is constructed on one of five patterns:

Pattern	Explanation	Example
1. SV	Subject + Verb	The ghost disappeared.
2. SVC	S + V + Complement	This is my husband.
3. SVO	S + V + Object	He makes watches.
4. SVOO	S + V + Indirect Object + Direct Object	He gave me this beautiful watch.
5. SVOC	S + V + Object + Complement	He made me happy.

It can easily be seen that the difference between one pattern and another lies in what, if anything, follows V: in other words it lies in the complementation, if any, of the verb. So what we are really concerned with is a difference in verb complementation or verb patterns. The patterns can be expanded and sub-divided as below.

7.1 THE SV PATTERNS

Pattern	Sub-division	Example
SV	1	The ghost disappeared.
	1a	I got up.
	2	The door opened.
	3	I watched, and listened.

SV 1: A good dictionary will indicate whether a verb can be used intransitively. Other verbs in SV 1 include *ache, come, fall, rise*.

1a: *Get* cannot be used intransitively without an adverbial particle (e.g. *up*) or adverbial adjunct (e.g. *into the car*). Other verbs requiring an adverbial include *lie* (e.g. *on the ground*) and *live* somewhere, at some time, somehow.

2: Obviously, someone or something caused the door to open. See SVO 1. Verbs that can be used similarly include *close, hurt, move, ring, stop, turn*.

3: I watched something (or someone), and *watch* can also be used in
SVO 1. The same applies to *ask, answer, drink, eat, forget, read,
write* and other verbs. But *listen, look* and *wait* will require a
preposition before they can be used transitively: see SVO 2.

7.2 THE SVC PATTERNS

Pattern	Sub-division	Example
SVC	1	This is a story.
	2	It is good.
	3	It was there. It was yesterday.

SVC 1: The verb in SVC is a copula, or linking verb. It can refer to an
unchanging state of affairs (e.g. *be, resemble, sound*), in which case
it will not occur in the continuous; or to a change of state (*become*),
in which case there is no restriction on the use of the continuous.
C in SVC 1 is a noun.

2: Here, C is an adjective. Verbs referring to a change of state include
the so-called inchoative verbs, as in *fall* (sick), *get* (tired), *go* (mad),
grow (old); *turn* (pale). Note that *get* is commonly used in SVC 2
but cannot occur in SVC 1.

3: Here, the complementation is an adverbial, usually of place,
though it could be of time (e.g. *The concert is at 8 o'clock*).

7.3 THE SVO PATTERNS

Pattern	Sub-division	Example
SVO	1	Someone opened the door.
	1a	He put his hand in his pocket.
	1b	He took something out.
	1c	He had a gun.
	2	I listened to his voice.
	3	I wanted to scream.
	4	I wanted him to go away.
	5	I longed for someone to come.
	6	I stopped trembling.
	7	I remember you(r) coming.
	8	I heard the bell ring.
	9	We heard a dog barking.
	10	We found the way blocked by a truck.
	11	I said (that) we should go to the police.
	12	I suggested that Dick (should) go.

13	I asked if (or whether) he had gone.
14	I wondered where you were.

SVO 1: Again, a good dictionary will indicate which verbs can be used transitively. They include *ask, answer, drink, eat* (see also SV 3), and *do, enjoy, make, manufacture* which are not used intransitively. All verbs in SVO 1, and SVO 1a and b can be put into the passive.

1a: An adverbial (or sometimes an adjective, e.g. *Put your desk straight*) is obligatory after *place* and *put;* also after *lay* as in *lay something on the ground.*

1b: Here, the adverb particle (*out*) can also come before the object, but not if the object is a personal pronoun.

1c: *Have* in the sense of 'possess', and *lack* (i.e. not have) will not be found in the passive.

2: *Listen, look* and *wait* can occur in SV 3. In SVO, a preposition is required, e.g *listen to/look at/wait for someone. Look after* only occurs in SVO. The same applies to *long for, part with* and *taste of.* V in SVO 2 is called a prepositional verb.

3: Other verbs complemented by *to* + infinitive are *agree, attempt, decide, fail, hope, need* (as a full verb) and *wish.* Note that *to* is optional after *dare*; and that (*can't*) *bear, begin, cease, continue, prefer, propose* can fit into SVO 3 or SVO 6, without any substantial change in meaning. *Deserve, forget, remember, try* can also be used in both SVO 3 and SVO 6, but with different meanings. Note that pattern SVO 3 can only be used when the two subjects are the same and the time references of the two verbs are the same (*I wanted. I was about to scream:* both past), or *I hope to go* (*I hope, I go:* both present). The pattern cannot be used, for example, to replace *I want you to go* or *I hope you will go* or *I hope I went to the right house.*

4: The object here is *him to go away.* I did not want *him.* The subject of *to go* is considered to be *he. Want* could be replaced by *expect, get, intend, mean, recommend, wish. Promise* fits into SVO 3 and 4; but in *I promise you to go away* the subject of *to go away* is *I.*

5: This is similar to SVO 4, but V is a prepositional verb as in SVO 2. *Long for* could be replaced by *arrange for, ask for, wait for.*

6: Other verbs complemented by *-ing* are *avoid, dislike, enjoy, fancy, finish,* (*can't*) *help, practise, suggest.* See notes on SVO 3. Note that *This wants* (or *needs*) *cleaning* means *This needs to be cleaned.*

7: Many of the verbs used in SVO 6 can also occur in SVO 7. The possessive form (*your, his, their, my, our, John's* etc.) is traditionally considered 'correct', though *you, him, them* etc. are now widely used. The possessive *its* might occur instead of *it*, but *that's* would be unacceptable, e.g. *I remember that happening to me once.*

8: Either the bare infinitive or the *-ing* could occur when V is *feel, hear, notice, see, watch*. But the *to*-infinitive is used in the passive: *The bell was heard to ring.*

9: See note on SVO 8. Only the *-ing* would occur in examples like *I found him smoking, They kept us waiting, We stopped the fire (from) spreading;* and in such examples the possessive form (*his, our* etc.) would be unacceptable.

10: Here, SVO is complemented by a past participle phrase (or clause). *Have* frequently occurs in this pattern, as in *I had my hair cut.*

11: Here O is a *that*-clause, which can be considered as an indirect statement. *That* is optional in short sentences on this pattern. Like *say* are *believe, don't doubt, feel, find, find out, note, notice, point out, wish.*

12: O is here a proposal for future action. Like *suggest* are *agree, ask, decide, insist, propose.*

13: Here O is an indirect Yes/No question; and *ask* could be replaced by *doubt, find out, forget, (don't) know, inquire, wonder.*

14: O is an indirect Wh-question, and *ask* is replaceable by *inquire, find out*, etc.

7.4 THE SVOO PATTERNS

Pattern	Sub-division	Example
SVOO	1	My father gave me this watch.
	2a	He gave this watch to me.
	2b	My mother made this scarf for me.
	3	Tell me about your home.
	4	Take care of your books.
	5	He persuaded us that we were wrong.
	6	Please inform me if you are coming.
	7	Tell me when you will arrive.

SVOO 1 & 2: Verbs fitting into SVOO 1 and 2a include *bring, fetch, grant, hand, lend, offer, owe, pass, pay, promise, read, sell, send, show, teach, tell, throw, write*. Those fitting into 1 and 2b include *book, build, buy, call, catch, change, choose, find, sleep, order, reserve, save, spare.*

2a: Note that *describe, explain, mention, say, suggest* fit into SVOO 2a but not into 1.

2b: *We provided blankets for the refugees* could be re-worded *We provided the refugees with blankets.*

3: Also in this pattern: *You asked me about my home. I informed him of the results. We congratulate you on your success.* Here, the prepositional phrase is closely linked with the verb, *ask, inform, congratulate.*

4: Here, the prepositional phrase is closely linked with the object, *care.* Similarly, *take advantage of something, pay attention to somebody.*

5: *Persuade* replaceable by *assure, convince, inform, remind, satisfy, tell.*

6 & 7: Also *remind* and *tell.*

7.5 THE SVOC PATTERNS

Pattern	Sub-division	Example
SVOC	1	We have appointed you Chairman.
	2	The islanders paint their houses white.
	3	You consider him guilty.
	4	I regard him as innocent.
	5	Did you mistake me for someone else?
	6	I consider it a shame/wrong to say that.
		I consider it a shame/wrong that he should be blamed.

SVOC 1: C is now the complement of O: *You have become Chairman.* In this pattern, we find *christen, crown, name, nominate.* With those verbs and *appoint*, two passives are possible: *You have been appointed (Chairman). A Chairman has been appointed.* We could replace *appointed* in the active voice by *made, declared, proclaimed, voted*; but then only one passive would be possible, i.e. *You have been made Chairman.*

2: The houses became white as a result. Note also *This will drive me mad. Keep your feet warm. Wipe the windows clean.*

3: We could insert *to be* after *consider;* and could re-word the example *You consider that he is guilty.* C could also be a noun, e.g. *a criminal.*

4: *Regard* replaceable by *count, describe, look on.*

5: *Mistake* replaceable by *take.*

6: In the pattern SVOC, O could be *-ing*, as in *I consider cheating dishonest*, but it could not be an infinitive or a that-clause. Instead, O is expressed by *it*, and the infinitive or *that*-clause comes after C, as in the example for SVOC 6.

7.6 ADJECTIVE PATTERNS

In SVC, when C is an adjective, it frequently has, and sometimes must have, its own complementation. Complementation is structurally optional in *I am afraid (of snakes)* but obligatory in *I was aware of the danger.*

Adjective patterns can take three basic forms:

1. Adjective + prepositional phrase
2. Adjective + *to*-infinitive, as in *afraid to jump*
3. Adjective + *that*-clause, as in *afraid (that) I might break my leg.*

We shall discuss the infinitive in the next chapter, and prepositions in Chapter 9. Meanwhile, note that in the pattern SVC, S is often an *It* that anticipates an infinitive or *that*-clause, as in *It is a pity to spoil your picture. It's very sad that you are leaving us.*

COMMENTARY AND DISCUSSION POINTS

This short chapter is the most abstract, and in that sense the most 'grammatical' in the book. Can you see any use for terminology such as SVOC in the classroom? Does it help **you** to see patterns more clearly?

If you answer *No* to the above, how do you hope to help students to see patterns? Modern linguistics suggests that students do not learn grammar, they acquire it – slowly, and perhaps subconsciously, developing an understanding of similarities and differences. However they do this, mastery of the language still involves perceiving, explicitly or otherwise, **patterns**. The reader may care to consider the question of how many different kinds of grammatical item can complete the sentence *They are ... (late, out, up to no good, policemen, ...).* What we start of by thinking is a very simple pattern, quickly becomes complicated if we choose to think about it. Somehow or other students have to master these patterns, knowing what is, and is not possible. Can you think of exercise types which might help them to understand the pattern, while perhaps avoiding unnecessary jargon?

8 Infinitive or - ing

The problems here are to know:

(a) whether to use the infinitive without *to* (*I must go*) or the *to*-infinitive (*I want to go*)

(b) whether to use the infinitive (*I refuse to go*; *I prefer to go*) or the verb ending in *-ing* (*I enjoy going, I prefer going*).

8.1 THE INFINITIVE OR -ING AFTER VERBS

These are mainly questions of plain fact. We must become familiar—through hearing and reading the language or through exercises—with a variety of patterns and constructions such as were set out in Chapter 7. We can only accept the facts:

(a) The bare infinitive is used after *do, does, did*; after *will, would, shall, should, can, could, may, might, might as well, had better, would rather, would sooner*; after *let*, as in *let go*, and *make*, as in *make do*; and in verb pattern SVO 8, *I heard the bell ring*.

(b) The *to*-infinitive occurs after *ought, used, have* and *be*; and in verb patterns SVO 3,4,5 and SVOC 6, as in Chapter 7.

(c) The *-ing* occurs in SVO 6,7 and 9.

(d) There is no option to replace the infinitive by *-ing* in *I hope to go*, or to replace the *-ing* by the infinitive in *I enjoy going*. The same is true of other such constructions which a good dictionary or reference grammar should indicate.

(e) We can say *We began to sing* or *We began singing* with no substantial change of meaning.

(f) We can say *I heard her sing* or *I heard her singing*, with a change of emphasis.

(g) We can say *I remembered to go* which does not mean the same as *I remembered going*.

(h) Only the *-ing* form, not the infinitive, follows a preposition or a prepositional verb (SVO 2). Thus *Let's talk about fishing. He earns his living by translating. Take these pills before and after eating. Kindly refrain from smoking.* etc. etc. Note *look forward to going* and *object to smoking* where *to* is a preposition, and *want to go*, where *to* is an infinitive marker, not a preposition. Note also the difference between *I'm used to waiting* and *I used to wait*.

We can trace three differences in meaning between the infinitive and the *-ing*. They may help to explain why the infinitive has become adopted in one pattern, while the *-ing* is adopted in another; and they can help us to decide which form to use when there is a choice.

Activity in general or activity in progress

The infinitive may refer either to the activity in general or to the act completed, in contrast with an *-ing* which refers to activity in progress. This distinction is similar to that between O and U in 5.1, thus:

I saw him jump   I saw him running away

Fig.32   Fig 33

Examples:

[1] I saw the man jump. (I O)
[2] I saw him running away. (I U)
[3] I heard the dog bark. (I O)
[4] I have often heard it bark. (S O)
[5] I heard it barking all night. (S U)

In those examples, *jump* is more precise than *jumping* if the speaker is referring to one completed act; *running* is better than *run* if the speaker is referring to the continuous action; *bark* refers to one sound, *barking* to a series of barks. Similarly, *I prefer to walk* could refer to the activity in general, while *I prefer walking* emphasises the continuous action. It is difficult to see such a distinction between *begin to run* and *begin running*: what is fairly certain is that *beginning running*, with its repetition of *-ings*, would be avoided. The chances are that after *begin, start, cease* and *continue* most users of English would choose the infinitive or the *-ing* by accident, or for the sake of euphony, rhythm or variety.

Activity having duration is, or can be, clearly emphasised by the *-ing* in *enjoy swimming. Do you mind waiting? Keep (on) walking. Go on reading.*

Activity in progress or new act

The *-ing* may refer to activity in progress, while the infinitive refers to a **new** act in a chain of events, as in

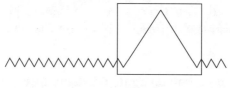

Fig 34

[6]   I like dancing. (= the activity)

[7]   Would you like to dance?

Like, love, hate, prefer can be followed by either the infinitive or the *-ing*, as in *I love to lie/I love lying in the sun*: perhaps to some speakers and writers *lying* rather than to *lie* would emphasise the duration of the sun-bathing, the continuous feeling of having the sun warming one's skin. But normally *would like, would love, would hate, would prefer* point to a new act in a chain of events and are followed by the infinitive. However, *would prefer* could be followed by *-ing* if it referred to activity in progress, having duration, as in *Which would you prefer, lying on the beach in the sun, or lying for days in a tiny spaceship?*

A distinction between new act (infinitive) and activity having duration (*-ing*) might be noticeable in the following pairs:

[8]   (a) It is a great pleasure to be with you tonight.

    (b) It is a great pleasure being with you tonight.

[9]   (a) The climbers made another attempt to reach the top.

    (b) The climbers made another attempt at reaching the top.

There is a greater difference between (a) and (b) in

[10] (a) We were interested to hear your news.

    (b) We are not interested in hearing gossip.

In [10] (a), we are interested in a new development. In [10] (b), we are not interested in the activity of listening to gossip. The difference is perhaps greater still in

[11] (a) Now let us try to turn the key to the right.

    (b) Now let us try turning the key to the right.

In [11] (a), *try to turn* would often be replaced in spoken English by *try and turn*, which refers to two separate acts: one, try; two, turn. In [11] (b), *turning* refers to a process; and the example means 'Let us experiment by turning the key to the right', in order to see if we can unlock the door that way. The difference is even greater in

[12] (a) They deserve to shoot first.

    (b) They deserve shooting first.

Here,(a) means they have earned the right to be the first to shoot while (b) means they ought to be shot before something else happens.

Move in a series or activity in progress

The infinitive points to a move forward in a series of events, while the *-ing* looks backwards to previous activity in progress or even to a previous act completed. Here, the two members of a pair may have quite different meanings:

[13] (a) I remembered to telephone the doctor.
(b) I remembered telephoning the doctor.

[13] (a) means: First I remembered what I had to do, then I telephoned. [13] (b) means: I telephoned the doctor, and remembered doing so. We could also say [13] (c) *I remembered having telephoned the doctor.* To be precise, I would use [13] (b) if I meant that I recalled the act of telephoning, and [13] (c) if I meant that I recalled that the act had been performed. There is a similar difference in

[14] (a) I usually forget to sign my letters.
(b) I shall never forget seeing Fujiyama by moonlight.

[14] (a) suggests that I forget that I have to sign my letters and therefore do not sign them, while [14] (b) suggests that I shall not forget an event that occurred in the past. Another such pair is

[15] (a) I regret to tell you that I shall be away.
(b) I regret telling you that I shall be away.

In [15] (a) I regret and now I tell you. In [15] (b) I (have) told you, and now I regret it. *I regret having told you* would emphasise the perfective interpretation of (b).

The *-ing* clearly refers to a process on which the speaker is looking back in *I stopped writing, finished working, gave up smoking.* On the other hand, the infinitive refers to a new act in *I stopped to write my name in the visitors' book.*

In *I stopped to write*, the infinitive is not a complementation of the verb. *I stopped* + infinitive can be analysed as SV plus an adverbial adjunct of purpose. Such an adjunct can be added to any of the verb patterns given in Chapter 7, so long as the verb refers to an action that can be performed voluntarily and purposefully. Thus:

[16] I stopped the car to look at the radiator.

[17] We sent her some flowers to thank her for the party.

The adverbial adjunct of purpose could be made clearer by inserting *so as*, or more formally *in order*, before the *to*-infinitive.

Compare example [16] above with

[18] I stopped the car to find that the radiator was almost empty.

where *to find* could be replaced by *and found* – a new act in the chain of events, expressing consequence rather than purpose.

8.2 INFINITIVE AFTER ADJECTIVES

As we saw in 7.6, an adjective acting as C in SVC (i.e. an adjective used predicatively) can be complemented by an infinitive. The meaning of this complementation is by no means always the same. We can distinguish at least seven different types, as the examples below and the re-wording of them will indicate:

1. *He is eager to go.* = He very much wants to go. There the adjective expresses an attitude, on the part of the person mentioned, towards something that has not happened, a possible future event; and the infinitive could not be replaced by *-ing*. Instead of *eager* we could say *able, anxious, determined, keen,* etc.

2. *He is certain to go.* = It is certain that he will go. Again, *to go* is a possible future event. But here *certain* is expressing the speaker's own attitude towards the future. (Note the difference between *Tom is certain to win* (the speaker is certain that he will) and *Tom is certain of winning* (Tom himself is certain that he will).)

3. *He is happy to go.* = He is happy because he is going. *He was happy to go,* because he went. *Happy* could be replaced by *delighted, fortunate, glad, proud, sorry,* etc. The infinitive could be replaced by an *-ing* clause that refers to continuing action, as in *He is very happy playing with his children again.*

4. *He is sensible to go.* = He is being sensible, or acting sensibly, by going; in other words, it is sensible of him to go. *Sensible* could only be replaced by adjectives which indicate a way of behaviour, e.g. *clever, kind, polite, rude, selfish, silly, wise.*

5. *He is quick to go on errands for me.* = He quickly agrees to go on errands. Instead of *quick* we could say *hesitant, prompt, slow, willing.*

6. *He is difficult to amuse.* = It is difficult for anyone to amuse him. The *-ing* could not replace the infinitive in that pattern, which could also be used for *easy, hard, hopeless, interesting.* We could use the pattern for an inanimate subject, as in *This car is easy to drive,* i.e. one can easily drive it.

7. If we replace *This car* in that last example by *It,* we get *It is easy to drive.* There, *it = this car.* But *It is easy to drive* could also mean *To drive* (or *Driving*) *is easy,* and in that case *It* stands for *to drive.*

8.3 INFINITIVE AFTER NOUNS

Generally speaking, the pattern *agree* (*arrange, decide, determine, fail, hesitate, offer, plan, promise, threaten, wish,* etc.) + *to*-infinitive (SVO 3) can be matched by *agreement* (*arrangement, decision, determination, failure, hesitation, offer, plan, promise, threat, wish,* etc.) + *to*-infinitive as in

[19] We agreed to share the profits; and our agreement to share the profits still stands.

Similarly *anxious* (*inclined, ready, reluctant, willing*) *to please* could be matched by *anxiety* (*inclination, readiness, reluctance, willingness*) *to please*. There are a few exceptions, e.g.

[20] We had hoped to finish this work by the end of this month, but there is no hope of doing so now.

[21] Some people like to read, others prefer to watch television, others have a preference for sitting and talking.

An infinitive can replace a relative clause after a noun, as in

[22] Here is an interesting book to read. (= an interesting book that you or anyone else can read)

[23] Here is another book for you to look at.

In [23] *for you to look at* means 'that you can look at', *for* being used to specify the subject of the infinitive clause. Other examples are:

[24] He is a man to trust. (or to be trusted)

[25] He was the first man to fly across the Atlantic.

An infinitive can similarly modify an indefinite pronoun:

[26] Would you like something to eat?

8.4 NOT TO, TO BE-ING, TO HAVE-ED

The negative, continuous and perfective of the infinitive are illustrated in the following dialogue:

[27] I'm sorry not to be able to stay longer. I'm sorry to be going so soon.
    – Yes, and I'm sorry you have to go. I'm sorry to have seen so little of you.

In *I am sorry to go* the subject of *am* is also the subject of *go*, and the time reference is the same in both parts of the sentence. However, instead of *I'm sorry (that) I saw/have seen so little of you*, we can use the perfect infinitive, *to have seen*. The perfect infinitive often gives trouble after *would like* and *would have liked*. Note these examples:

> [28] (a) I would like (now) to see that exhibition (now).
> (b) I would like (now) to have seen it (before now).
> (c) I would have liked (then) to see it (then).
> (d) I would have liked (then) to have seen it (before then).

8.5 INFINITIVE OR -ING AS SUBJECT, OBJECT OR COMPLEMENT

We have already seen that both the infinitive and the *-ing* can act as object of a verb; but certain verbs take only the infinitive as the object, while others take only the *-ing*. Both forms can act as subject of a sentence, as in

> [29] To learn (or learning) a new language is difficult.

However, the *-ing* is more likely to begin a sentence than the infinitive; and *It*, as subject, frequently anticipates the infinitive, e.g.

> [30] It is difficult to learn a new language.

Both forms could act as a complement of *be*, as in

> [31] My greatest pleasure is lying (or to lie) in the sun.

8.6 -ING CLAUSES

Lying in the sun, as in [31] can be described as an *-ing* clause in which the continuous process of sun-bathing is emphasised. It is similarly emphasised in

> [32] Lying in the sun like this, I feel perfectly at ease.

There *I* is assumed to be the subject of *lying*. I am lying here, and I feel perfectly at ease. Note that

> [33] *Lying here on the sand, the sun feels very warm.

is unacceptable, because it is not the sun that is lying. But there would be no objection to

> [34] Running to the water, I feel the sand burning beneath my feet,

where it is clear that I am running and the sand is burning.

While the link between the *-ing* form of the verb and the continuous is strong, and often obvious, there are occasions when an *-ing* clause bears no relation to the continuous aspect at all. We have already seen that it is difficult to imagine a single act of jumping in an uncompleted state. Yet there is only one quick jump in:

[35] Jumping into his car, he drove off in pursuit.

There, we are concerned with two consecutive acts – he jumped, then he drove; and the first is reported in a subordinate position in the sentence. This throws the spotlight onto the action reported by the finite verb (*drove*). Note that in [35], as the jumping came first, the *-ing* clause must precede the main clause. But in

[36] Ignoring the traffic lights, he raced in pursuit,

the *-ing* refers to a process in which the driver is engaged as he goes along, as well as expressing an action that is formally subordinated to *he raced*. The actions here are not consecutive, as they are in [35]: they are simultaneous, and ignoring the traffic lights could either precede or follow the main clause.

The *-ing* can even be used with verbs which would rarely, if ever, be used in the continuous, thus:

[37] Knowing Dick so well, I can thoroughly recommend him.

However, a difference in the use of the *-ing* in [36] and [37] becomes apparent when we expand the examples as follows:

[36a] Ignoring the traffic lights as he was (ignoring the traffic lights)

[37a] Knowing Dick as I do (know him)

A confusion often occurs between *amusing* and *amused, interesting* and *interested*, and similar pairs that can be used adjectivally. The problem can easily be resolved in the following way:

[38] (a) This story amuses/bores/fascinates/interests/me.
     (b) It is amusing/boring/fascinating/interesting.
     (c) I am amused by/bored by/fascinated by/interested in it.

Whether the *-ing* form of the verb is what is traditionally called a present participle or a gerund is often an academic question of no great importance. However, there are occasions when it is helpful to distinguish between two kinds of *-ing,* calling one a participle, the other a gerund, for convenience.

[39] Standing in the sun I feel too hot.

[40] Standing in the sun makes me giddy.

Standing in [39], agreeing with *I*, could be called a participle. *Standing* in [40], equivalent to a noun, could be called a gerund.

Running in a *running stream* could be called a participle; and *running* and *stream* are equally stressed. In *running shoes* (i.e. shoes used for running) it could be called a gerund; and *running* bears a strong stress while *shoes* does not.

If in a noun phrase there is a series of modifiers coming before the head-word, then a participle used as an adjective would come before a gerund, as in *This charming French writing desk*.

8.7 HAVING-ED, HAVING BEEN-ED

These constructions sometimes seem difficult to use, though they need not be as the following pairs illustrate:

[41] (a) I have travelled round the world and have made many friends.
(b) Having travelled round the world, I have made etc.

[42] (a) You have been invited to the reception formally and you ought to send a formal reply.
(b) Having been invited to the reception formally, you ought etc.

[41] (a) and [41] (b) have the same meaning; so have [42] (a) and [42] (b).

COMMENTARY AND DISCUSSION POINTS

In this whole chapter Close exemplifies one of the principal features of his approach – he is trying to find an **underlying similarity of pattern, which allows generalisation**. Do you believe he succeeds in finding a basic, fundamental difference between the infintive and -*ing* form?

The chapter represents another version of a theme which recurs throughout this book – Close believes that it is useful to find generalisations, even if they have then to be qualified, or exceptional uses noted. Do you agree?

What view do you think students often have of grammar – a collection of isolated, separate items which simply have to be mastered? Rules with exceptions? A combination of powerful rules and other items which simply have to be learned? How would **you** categorise grammar? Does your view of it influence what you do in the classroom?

It is certainly true that some grammatical generalisations are much more fundamental (for example Close's Primary Distinctions of chapter 2), and failure to master them will leave you totally at sea in understanding English. And (explicit or implicit) understanding of those distinctions is essential. There are other useful hints which are generalisable, but not fully so. In addition there are items which simply need to be learned. It must surely be helpful to students to be aware of these different kinds of grammatical information.

9 Prepositions, Adverb Particles and Phrasal Verbs

9.1 PREPOSITIONS

The prepositions express relationships in space between one thing and another, and relationships in time between events. They might be considered basically as applications of the ideas contained in the scheme:

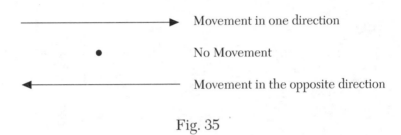

Fig. 35

to something having no, or an unspecified, dimension; to something having one dimension; having two dimensions; or three dimensions. In space, let us call something with no, or unspecified dimension, a point; with one dimension, a line, two dimensions, a surface, three, a space or area. (Be careful to distinguish between 'space (not time)' and 'a space, something having volume'.) In time, we can imagine a point of time, or a period. In using the prepositions we are concerned not so much with objective measurements, i.e. with the actual dimensions of the things to which we are referring, as with **how we imagine them to be at the time of speaking**. Thus we can imagine a town as a point on the map, as a surface to go across, or as a space we live in or walk through. Moreover, a point itself, seen through a microscope, may appear to have surface which can be covered or space which can be penetrated.

It is possible to fit a great number of usages into this scheme, and there is much to be said, in teaching the prepositions, for beginning with those usages which fall into a scheme of this kind easily. On the other hand, many usages are very difficult to systematise. That is not surprising. Some of the relationships we want to express are very complex. We express them by little words whose full meaning could only be explained in long circumlocutions. Moreover, the number of these little words is limited, and each may have to serve a variety of purposes. Nevertheless, the use of prepositions in English can be remarkably, almost geometrically, precise, and students would be well advised to be as clear about them as they can, without forcing natural usage into an artificial framework.

9.2 NO, OR UNSPECIFIED, DIMENSION: TO, AT, FROM

Movement in the direction of a point is expressed by *to*; in the opposite direction, by *from*. Imagine two things, X and Y, occupying two different positions; and imagine the position of Y to be a point or to be of unspecified dimension. If X moves so as to occupy more or less the same position as Y, then we say that X moves *to* Y. So X is now *at* Y. If we now remove X, we take it *from* Y. Thus

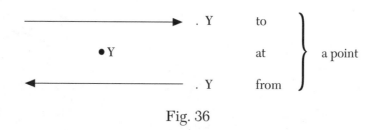

Fig. 36

Remember that *to* and *from* express **movement**; *at*, **no movement**. All three can be applied to a point both in space and in time: *This train goes from London to Edinburgh in four hours, stopping only at York. Your lesson is from nine to (or till) ten in the morning: It starts promptly at nine.* (But *Your lesson will last till ten* – not *to*, when *from* is omitted.)

Other examples of *to, at* and *from*:

(a) *Go to bed. Listen to me. Does this book belong to you? Best wishes to you all. I passed, thanks to you. Be kind to animals, don't* be *cruel to them. Stick to your principles.* Note that the infinitive marker *to* frequently points **forward** to a fresh act in the course of events: see 8.1

(b) *I live at this address, at number 30. At what time shall we meet? I'm busy at the moment.* Notice especially:

   (i) the idea of **stationary relationship with unspecified dimension** in *I'm sitting at a desk, at a table, at the window; I'm standing at the door.* Contrast: *Your book is on, or in, the desk, on the table. Who stuck that paper on the window?; There's a name painted on the door.*

   (ii) the same idea applied to a **general concept** (see p42): *at work, at play, at rest, at fault, at peace, at war* (cp, *in the war*, to emphasise the period, and also to specify which war), *at sea* (cp. *on the sea*, i.e. on the surface, and *in the sea*, i.e. in the volume of water), *at night* (cp. *in the night*, to emphasise the period, and either to specify which night, or to distinguish night from day).

(iii) concentration on the **final point** of the movement: *aim at, arrive at, laugh at, shoot at, throw at.* Note: *throw the ball to me,* i.e. in my direction, not *at me,* so as to hit me. Similarly, *point to the blackboard,* but *don't point at other people – it's rude.*

(c) *How far is the bus stop from here? Let's escape from it all. Tell me the worst, don't hide it from me. No one can prevent me (from) finding out. To be absent from work.*

9.3 Towards, As Far As

To envisages completed movement and suggests that X actually reaches Y, or will reach Y unless prevented. Movement in the direction of Y, without the idea of completion, is expressed by *towards.* This applies only to space, though we sometimes say *towards (six o'clock)* to mean *about* or *nearly* then. To emphasise the length of the journey to Y, which is eventually reached, we say *X goes as far as Y.*

9.4 Till (or Until), Since

As far as is used only for space. To emphasise length of time, eventually concluded, we say *till* or *until* the final point. *If you want a walk, I'll come with you as far as the shops, but I am not ready yet—I shall be busy till five o'clock. Since,* means 'in the progress of time from a specified point in the past until the speaker's point of primary concern', whether SPPC is present or past, *I have not seen him since Thursday. Yesterday was the hottest day since 1925.*

9.5 (Away) From, Far, Near

From (with space) is reinforced by *away,* which stresses the idea of the separation of the two positions held by X and Y. Thus *X is at Y. Now it moves away from Y.* When X occupies a different position from Y, and is stationary, then we say

| X is | so many inches (miles, etc.) some distance, a long way not far | (away) from Y. |

If Y is mentioned, *from* must precede it, and *away* is optional. To emphasise the **shortness** of the distance between X and Y, we say *X is near Y.*

Note that in short sentences *far* will often occur in the interrogative (Is it far?) and negative (It isn't far), but is avoided in a short affirmative sentence (It's a long way), unless *far* is modified by an adverb (It's quite far).

9.6 FOR

To express the object or purpose of the *to* movement, or to indicate the person or thing affected by it, we can use *for*. Thus:

(a) *The train for Paris* (the train that is planned to go to Paris), *a ship bound for Rio, We're just starting off / out for the north, going for a holiday. Go for a walk, a swim, a drive, for pleasure, for what purpose? What for? We shall be out for dinner. We're having chicken for dinner.*

(b) *This is a present for you* — *I bought it to give to you. And this is for John. I'm doing this for you* (for your benefit, or on your behalf). *I'm asking (calling, looking, longing, sending) for you* — the object and purpose of those actions. *I'm sorry for you* (I'm giving you my sympathy). Notice the extension of this usage in *I'm for you* (giving you my support), *I'm for the motion* (giving my support to a proposal in a debate).

(c) With time, *for* + a measurement of time can indicate the proposed, expected or completed length of the period during which an action takes place: *We shall be staying in Scotland for three weeks. You've been learning English for six years. You were at school for twelve years. We walked for two hours. I shall love you for ever.*

For can also indicate exchange; e.g. *I bought this for ten dollars. May I change it for a slightly smaller one? You couldn't get anything smaller for love nor money. Thank you for your help.*

9.7 OF & FROM

From, like *to*, basically expresses a physical movement, clearly traceable. The idea of *from* can be expressed in a more general, abstract way by *of*, to indicate origin or one of the relationships defined below. Examine the following pairs:

[1]   (a)   This cupboard was made from an old wooden packing-case (a specific, clearly traceable transition).   (b)   It is therefore made of wood. (The transition from substance to object is less obvious, more general.)

[2] (a) These are all vegetables from my garden.   (b) They are the fruits of the earth, results of my labours.

[3] (a) Fill the bucket from the well.   (b) The bucket's full of water.

[4] (a) Take some paper from my writing-pad.   (b) Have you taken a piece of my writing-pad?

[5] (a) Have a chocolate – take one from the bottom layer.   (b) I won't have another of yours—you have one of mine.

[6] (a) I could make you a vase from this lump of clay.   (b) Are you making a fool of me, making fun of me?

An important function of *of* is to express the relationship between the part and the whole: *some of all, a quarter of an hour*. Variations of this are: the relationships between the member and the body to which that member belongs (*the leg of a chair, the top of the stairs, the secretary of the club*); between a quality and something possessing it (*the beauty of the landscape*); between a condition and something in that condition (*the health of a nation*); between an aspect and the thing we are considering (*a view of the summit*: cp. *a view from the summit*); and so on.

Of is like the line in a fraction in mathematics. In $^3/_8, ^8/_3, ^x/_y, ^y/_x$, the line tells us the relationship between 3 and 8, x and y, so long as we understand the significance of the order of the symbols dependent on which word comes before *of* and which after it. So there is a difference between *the book of the film* (the film came first) and *the film of the book* (the book came first). Both of *This is the century of the Car*, and *This is the car of the Century*, have a clear meaning, but the meanings are quite different.

9.8 BY, BEYOND, PAST, BEFORE, AFTER

Look again at Fig. 36. Suppose we alter the position of the arrows and the small circle, so that the diagram looks like this:

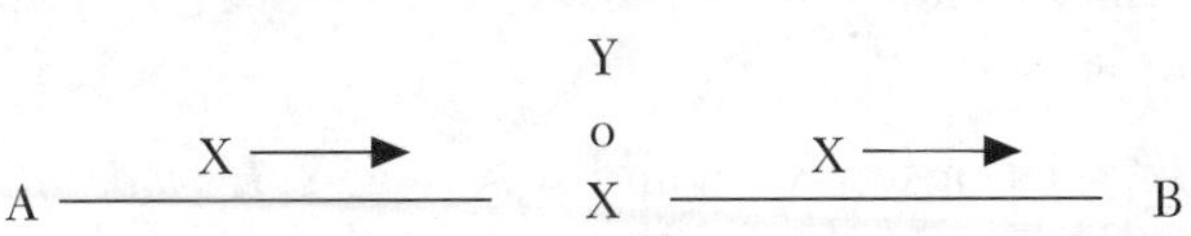

Fig. 37

The movement now is in one direction only, although it may stop at o. Suppose X moves, in space, from A to B. In the process, *X goes by the point Y*. At o, X is stationary: it is then *by the point Y*. Notice that it goes not only as far as Y but also *beyond* it. To emphasise the fact that, in going by Y, X also goes beyond it, we can say that *X goes past Y*.

In time, the first arrow in Fig 37 begins at A, which is *before Y*, and ends *by Y*. In this sense, *by* can be analysed to mean in the progress of time ending about but not later than the point of time mentioned. Compare *by* with *till* in the following pair of sentences:

[8] (a) I shall not be ready till five o'clock. (my not being ready will extend through a period ending at that point, when I shall be ready)
(b) I shall not be ready by five o'clock. (I shall not be ready in a period ending at five)

Note that the verb in (a) must be one that refers to activity that can extend through a period of time, e.g. *I waited till five*. On the other hand, the verb in (b) can be a point-of-time verb, e.g. *We shall leave by five*.

Fig. 37, B is *after* Y; in other words, at B, time has gone past Y, and in that sense *B is past Y*; thus *it is half past eleven, past my bedtime*. Continuous progress of time, past Y, then past a new point, Z, etc. can be said to go on *by day* and *by night*.

It may be stretching the imagination to fit *by* as an expression of means or agency into this scheme. If only for convenience and to complete the picture, I would classify this aspect of *by* as a relationship represented by the second part of the movement in Fig 37. It is easy enough to see that the train goes from London to Edinburgh *by* York. The next step is to see that the traveller goes from London to Edinburgh *by York*, and *by train*. In Fig. 37, Y is the means *by* which B is attained. (Compare this with *with*, 9.18.) This could enable us to account for usages on the pattern of *by means of, by electricity*, and also *a book by Conan Doyle*, i .e. the medium by which the book was created. I would not pretend that it accounts for certain other usages, such as *This room measures 6 metres by 4*.

Examples of *by*:

(a) in space, continuous movement passing Y: *I always go by the post-office on my way to the station.*

(b) in space, fixed relationship with and very near Y: *He was sitting by the fire, by the open window, by his mother, by himself* (i.e. alone). For *walking along by the river*, see 9.11.

(c) in space – means or agency: *We'll manage this somehow – by hook or by crook. To travel by car, by air, by sea. To send a message by ordinary mail, by telephone, by radio. To learn something by heart, by chance. Material made by hand, by machinery. 'Ode to a Nightingale', by John Keats.*

(d) in time, ending near, and not past, Y: *'Cobbler, cobbler mend my shoe, Get it done by halfpast two.' The concert will be over by ten.*

(e) in time, passing one stage after another: *To avoid being seen, they travelled by night, and lay hidden during the day.*

9.9 ROUND, ABOUT

X can go round Y:

(a) like a fence round a tree:

Fig. 38

(b) like a yacht sailing round a buoy:

Fig. 39

(c) like a man walking round a corner:

Fig. 40

Around has the same meaning as *round*, and can be substituted for it for the sake of rhythm, e.g. to avoid two stressed syllables coming together. In space, *about*, as a concrete expression of (a), is now out of fashion. Shakespeare's *Julius Caesar* said: *'Let me have men about me that are fat.'* In modern English, this would be *'I must have men around me'*, or *'round about me'* if one wanted to reinforce the idea of having such men on every side. In the abstract, *about* commonly suggests **moving in any direction**, or **being in any position, in**

the vicinity of the point; e.g. *think, talk, know, dream about the subject; tell me all about it; don't worry about it; what is it about?* A *book, or a lecture, about mountaineering* suggests a general treatment of the subject and freedom to wander a little from the point; whereas *a book, or a lecture, on new techniques in rock-climbing*, suggests concentration on a clearly defined field. In time, *I'll be there about six o'clock* is a common usage, expressing the idea of (a). We can also say *I'll be there around six o'clock*.

9.10 One Dimension: To, On, Off, From

Now apply the scheme to a line:

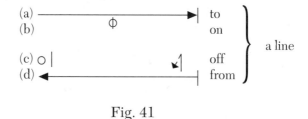

Fig. 41

Examples:

(a) *This road leads to the river, to the coast, to the frontier.*

(b) *London is on the River Thames. Brighton is on the coast. I'm on my way home. Am I on the right road for Y? Never stand on the edge of a cliff* (Note, however: *Will there be a customs examination at the frontier?* i.e. at the point on the frontier where our road crosses it.)

(c) *You're not on the right road for X – but you're not far off it. The 'Titanic' was wrecked off the coast of Greenland. A man was killed last night when his car skidded off the road and crashed into a tree.*

(d) *Refugees fleeing from the frontier. Stand away from the edge.*

9.11 Along, Across

When we say *X is on the road to Y*, we are more concerned with X's position than with its movement. To emphasise the idea of movement following the course before it, we say *X is moving along the road to Y*. Thus:

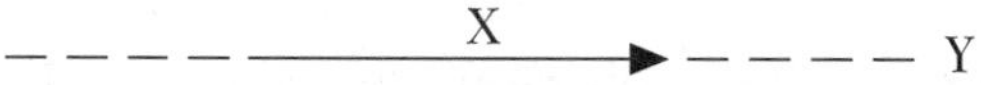

$$ - - - - \underline{\quad\quad\quad}^{X}\!\!\longrightarrow - - - - \ Y $$

Fig. 42

Apply figure 37 to a line, either thus:

Fig. 43

or thus:

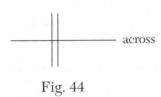

Fig. 44

Fig. 43 could represent *a man walking by (or beside) a river*, or *walking along by*, or *along beside*, it; or, at o, *a man standing by*, or *beside the river*.

Fig. 44 could represent *a road running across the frontier*, or *a tree lying across the railway line*.

9.12 BEHIND, IN FRONT OF

In the following situation

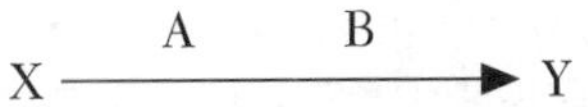

Fig. 45

A is behind B, and B is in front of A. This applies both when the arrow represents the line of vision of a speaker at X, and when it represents a line of advance along which A and B are moving in the direction indicated.

9.13 TWO DIMENSIONS: ON (OR ONTO), ON, OFF

Movement in the direction of a surface, and reaching it, is expressed by *on*. To emphasise movement towards and then position on the surface, or the effort required to complete that process, we say *onto*. (This is sometimes written *on to*, which might be confused with the *on to* in *We walked on to Rome*.) To indicate that X (moving or stationary) covers some or all of the surface Y, we use *on*. The opposite of *onto*, and the negative of *on* (i.e. *not on*) is *off*.

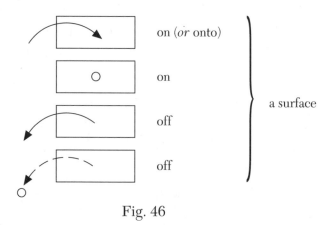

Fig. 46

The surface can be horizontal (e.g. the floor, the ceiling); it can be vertical (a wall); or lateral (a side). Examples:

(a) *Have you put the bread on the table?* (movement, but *onto* unnecessary). *This suitcase is terribly heavy. Can you help me lift it onto the bed?* (*onto* emphasing movement in that direction, then placing on the surface); *Hang the pictures on the wall.*

(b) *Is the bread on the table? How can I sleep with this suitcase on the bed? Don't run on the flower-beds. Keep on the right side of the law.*

(c) *Help me get this suitcase off the bed again. Keep your feet off the chairs.*

As we noticed with *talk about* v *talk on*, *on* concentrates on a more clearly defined field: a field is a surface having length and breadth. Moreover, while *X is at Y* suggests that X occupies more or less the same position as Y, without specifying dimension, *X is on Y* indicates that X covers some if not all of the actual surface of Y, or is supported by it, or is attached to it. Example: *There was no policeman at the spot where the accident occurred, but the police were on the spot within two minutes*, i.e. they were standing on the actual scene of the accident. A fish, nibbling *at your bait*, is not yet *on your hook*. From all this, it should be easy to understand *a hat on one's head, a house on the top of the hill, riding on horseback, standing on one's own feet* – and hence *to travel on foot*.

With time, note: *at six o'clock on a sunny day in June*, *on* covering a division of time intermediate between that associated with *at* and that with *in*. Similarly, *on Monday, on Tuesday*, etc., *on the morning (afternoon, evening) of the third day.* Observe the difference between *Where were you on the morning of November 19th?* i.e. on that precise date, and *On November 19th, I was working at my office in the morning, but went home feeling unwell in the afternoon.*

On can therefore be used:

(a) with reference to a line.

(b) to show X moving towards, and reaching a surface, horizontal or vertical.

(c) to show X at rest, partially or wholly covering Y, or supported by it.

(d) with reference to time, in establishing the date of an event, precise to the day of the week or month.

Upon is sometimes substituted for *onto* (movement) and *on* (rest) in dignified or poetic language, for the sake of rhythm, or to suggest 'firmly on' or 'high up on'. *Upon* occurs in certain fixed expressions, like the exclamatory *upon my word; upon my soul*, though these are now out of fashion and seem very dated.

Other relationships with a surface are:

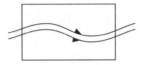

Fig. 47

A road running across the plain.

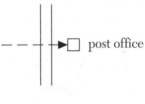

Fig. 48

The post office is just across the road.

9.14 THREE DIMENSIONS; IN (OR INTO), IN (OR INSIDE), OUT OF, OUTSIDE

In space, movement in the direction of a space and penetrating it is expressed, simply, by *in*; but to mark the emphasis comparable to that expressed by *onto* we say *into* a space. To indicate that X occupies some or all of the space Y, we use *in*. The opposite of *into* is *out of*. The negative of the preposition *in* (i.e. *not in*) is *outside*. To **emphasise** the idea of *not outside* we use *inside*.

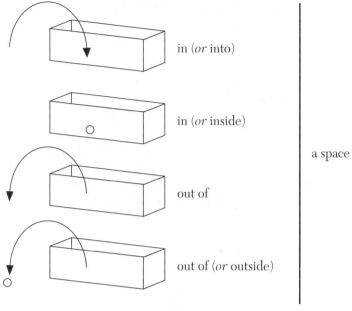

Fig. 49

Examples:

(a) *Put these books in your suitcase* (movement, but *into* unnecessary). *People started running into the building* (*into* emphasising the complete movement, and also necessary to avoid confusion with running in the building which might suggest running inside, not outside it).

(b) *Is my book in your suitcase? Shakespeare was born in England, in Warwickshire. I don't like swimming in muddy water, nor in the dark. Wait inside the car till the rain stops.*

(c) *They all rushed out of the building again when the explosion occurred.*

(d) *Outside the house, the crowd watched anxiously.*

9.15 IN, WITHIN

Whereas *X is on Y* suggests that Y supports X, *X is in Y* suggests that Y encloses X: in other words, Y has limits which hold X. Imagine and demonstrate the difference between *I place this coin on my hand* and *What have I got in my hand?* Such limits may enclose a surface-area; but in saying *in this area (district, region), in this city, in Africa,* etc., the emphasis is not on the supporting surface but on the space enclosed by certain limits. Emphasis on the idea of **in certain limits and not outside them** is contained in the word *within,* which can be used for space (*within an area*) or time (*within six days*).

There are many metaphorical applications of the above uses of *in.* Examples: *To be in debt, in love, in trouble, in good health. This book is written in English.*

9.16 IN, DURING

In is used with a period of time, thus: *Classes start in October. He was born in 1846, in the nineteenth century. Rome was not built in a day*, i.e. it was not built within the limits of twenty-four hours. *I'll see you in ten minutes* (or *ten minutes' time*), means 'I'll see you at the end of ten minutes.' Note that the word *time* is only added to that last example when we mean 'so many minutes (hours, etc.) from now'. *He ran a mile in four minutes* means that his running took exactly that time. *During* is used to indicate the continuance or extent of a period, or of an event or series of events occurring within that period; e.g. *The entrance examinations will be held during September. During the examination*, i.e. while it is in progress, *you cannot leave the room*. The difference between *in* and *during* might be shown thus:

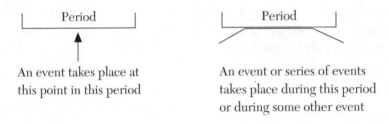

An event takes place at this point in this period

An event or series of events takes place during this period or during some other event

Fig. 50

Comparable with *passing by a point*, or *across a line or surface*, we have *through a space or period*, thus:

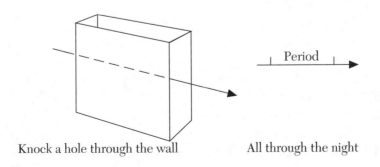

Knock a hole through the wall

All through the night

Fig. 51

9.17 UP, DOWN; OVER, UNDER, UNDERNEATH; ABOVE, BELOW, BENEATH

Up (↑) and *down* (↓) should raise no difficulty; nor should

over   and   under

Compare *a roof over one's head*, i.e. providing cover or protection, with *a hat on one's head*, i.e. touching, and supported by, its surface; similarly, compare *a fly on the ceiling*, i.e. attached to it and *a dog under the table*, i.e. covered by it. The idea of being physically covered up can be emphasised by *underneath* e.g. *I found this important letter underneath a pile of newspapers. Above* stresses the idea of at a higher point or on a higher level; *below*, a lower point or level. A swimmer has to keep his head *above water*; what is important is that his mouth should be at a higher level than the water's surface. A skin-diver must be careful not to go *below* a certain depth otherwise the pressure at that lower level will cause him serious injury. A man can be *above me* or *below me* in rank, without being *over me* or *under me*, i.e. without directly controlling me or having to obey my orders. Emphasis on the idea of the lowness of the level is contained in *beneath*, especially in poetic and metaphorical expressions, as in *beneath the waves, beneath contempt.*

Over and *under* express both rest and motion. *Over* often expresses the following movement:

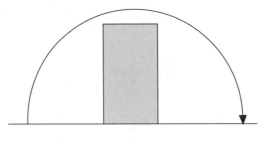

Fig. 52

and often emphasises the idea of having arrived at the other side of an obstacle: *The cow jumped over the moon* and *You're over the line*, i.e. you've crossed it.

9.18 RELATIONSHIPS BETWEEN FORCES—WITH, WITHOUT, AGAINST

Now consider relationships between the forces represented by the arrows at the beginning of this chapter:

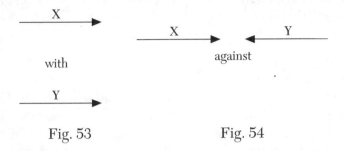

Fig. 53   Fig. 54

In Fig. 53, *X is going with* Y. The negative of this statement is, of course, *X is not going with* Y: in other words, it is going *without* Y. Physically, the opposite of it (Fig. 54), is *X is going against* Y. Note *Come and sit by (or with) me; and then come with me to the concert*. Note also the instrumental *with*, and compare it with the *by* of means or agency. When you *write with a pen*, your hand and pen proceed together.

On the other hand, when you *swim against the current*, you and the current are in conflict. Even when you are *leaning against the wall*, there is a force against you: if that force is not strong enough, the wall collapses. *One fights against temptation, struggles against fierce opposition, produces arguments against one's opponents in a debate*. Nevertheless — partly, perhaps, for reasons connected with the derivation of the word *with* — one can still *fight with an adversary, struggle with a problem, argue with one's wife*: in such cases, one might imagine oneself and one's adversary proceeding together in the same movement, the same furious dance. But notice how this apparent confusion is clarified in the following example: in a game of bridge, North and South are playing with East and West. To make it clear who are partners and who are opponents, we say *North is playing with South, East is playing with West, and North and South are playing together against East and West*.

9.19 OTHER RELATIONSHIPS: BETWEEN, AMONG

X may stand or move *between two objects*, Y and Z, thus:

Y   (X   or   ↓   X)   Z

or *among more than two.*

Note I can divide this money *between you two* or distribute it *among (or amongst) you all*. In popular speech, *between* is often used for more than two. Even speakers consciously endeavouring to restrict *between* to two things only, would feel it unnatural to do so when discussing, for example, *the difference between various factors*, although in such a situation they might be thinking of the difference between only two factors at a time, i.e. between X and Y, and then between X (or Y) and Z.

9.20 LIKE, AS

In comparing one thing with another, we may find that *X is like Y*, or *unlike* it. A distinction is made, and still insisted upon by grammarians, between the preposition *like*, which indicates a relationship between objects, and the conjunction *as* introducing a subordinate, finite clause e.g. *John walks just like his father*, but *He walks just as his father used to (walk)*. Most grammarians would consider it 'incorrect' to use *like* in the second example, although it is becoming common among native speakers of English. Nor would traditional grammar classify *as* as a preposition – even in the phrase you have just read. Yet it is difficult not to consider *as* with the other little words in this chapter. However grammarians may classify *as*, the student will no doubt want to see the difference between, say, *He spoke to me like a father* (comparison) and *He wrote to me as my legal adviser* (in that role or capacity).

9.21 FACTORS INFLUENCING CHOICE OF PREPOSITION

Subjective Choice

One can arrive *at* a point on the map (*We arrived at the station five minutes early*), arrive *on* what one sees as a surface (*We arrived on the platform just as the train was coming in*), or arrive *in* a space (*We arrived in London late last night*). One can be *on a chair* or *in a chair*, according to whether the speaker has in mind the surface of the seat or the space contained by the seat, the back and the arms. One can be *in bed* on a cold night, or can rest *on the bed* on a hot afternoon. One can drive *across London*, or *through it*, according to whether one sees it as a surface-area or a conglomeration of streets and buildings.

As we saw in chapter 1, some grammar is a matter of fact but often the speaker has a choice between two or more correct expressions. The choice is made by the speaker, at the moment of language use dependent on how the speaker conceptualises the situation at that moment. Subjective factors and perception influence the speaker's choice as well as objective factors.

Influence of Latin and Greek

The Latin prepositions — *ab* (= from), *ad* (= to), *cum* (= with), *de* (= from), *ex*, *e* (= from, out of), and the Greek *sym* (= with) — absorbed into English words as prefixes, tend to attract the English prepositions which are supposed to be equivalent in meaning. Thus: *absent from, adhere to, communicate with, different from, exempt from, sympathise with*. With *different* there would appear to be a conflict between etymology, which requires the preposition *from,* and the tendencies in modern English which I am trying to trace in this chapter. Many native English-speakers, uninhibited by a strict grammatical teaching, point from one thing to another, and remark that *this is different to that*. That is natural and logical, even if it is incorrect by traditional rules. With words of this kind, be careful to observe what the object of the prefix is: for example, in *The dishonest cashier absconded with the cash,* absconded means 'go or hide away from somewhere', and in that example *with* is a straightforward prepositional use.

Mechanical Association

While the foregoing paragraphs in this chapter may have provided some form of systematisation for the English prepositions, a great many usages can only be mastered by mechanical association, especially where the idea of movement or position in space is very weak or absent altogether. I can offer no 'explanation' for such associations as *afraid of nothing, believe in miracles, suffer from an illness, congratulate you on your success*. Students must not be surprised if they find that in some of these purely mechanical associations even native-English usage can be uncertain and conflicting. In any case, an important element in English grammatical usage is knowing what prepositions are used in the patterns discussed in Chapter 7. Carefully noticing usage, copying out the verb or adjective **together with a prepositional phrase attached to it**, and noting the examples given in a good dictionary, are perhaps the only ways of establishing these associations, though I hope this chapter will have made many of them clearer.

9.22 PREPOSITIONS IN RELATIVE CLAUSES, AND QUESTIONS

All the prepositions (except *during* and *since*) can fit into the following patterns:

(a) I am referring to the question of your debts.

(b) That is the question to which I am referring.

(c) That's the question I'm referring to.

(b) is more formal; and, in spoken English, sounds clumsy and unnatural; (c), more colloquial, though becoming increasingly acceptable in writing. In the interrogative, note

(d) To what are you referring? (note as for (b)).

(e) What are you referring to? (note as for (c)).

During and since are acceptable in patterns (a), (b) and (d), but not in (c) and (e). Example: *Since when have you been in charge? During which months does India have its heaviest rainfall?*

9.23 Adverbial Particles

The preposition separated from its object, as above, must be distinguished from the adverbial particle, which indicates a movement or position in space or time without direct reference to an object. Most of the prepositions can be used as adverbial particles, but not all of them can be. Those that can be are shown below:

Preposition	**Adverbial Particle**
Walk across the street.	How can we get across?
I saw him coming along the road.	Come along.
Who is that behind you?	Don't be left behind.
My cabin is below the main deck.	I'm going below.
I passed by your window.	Why pass by?
Go down the hill.	Go down.
Keep in front of me.	Keep in front.
Get in the car.	Get in.
Stay inside the house.	Stay inside.
Get off the bus.	Get off quickly.
Get on the bus.	Get on again.
Go out of the room.	Go out.
Stay outside the house.	Stay outside.
Jump over the gate.	Jump over.
Drive past the school.	Drive past.
Since New Year.	I haven't seen him since.
Get through the hole.	How can I get through?
Crawl under the rope.	Can you crawl under/ underneath?
Run up the hill again.	Run up again.

The adverbial particles thus express movement or positions in space and time similar to those expressed by the corresponding prepositions. The following are not used as adverbial particles: *to, at, from, towards, till, for, of, into, during, with, without, against*, though the nouns that follow can sometimes be omitted and understood, as in *Are you for the motion, or against?* Note also *come to* (recover from unconsciousness), *go without, do without – something*. On the other hand, there are two important particles with no corresponding prepositions, namely *away* and *back*, e.g. *Don't go away. Please come back.*

9.24 ADVERB PARTICLES WITH OTHER MEANINGS

In addition to the basic meanings already given, *on, off, in, out* and *up* have the following special meanings:

On indicates movement forwards, continuity, e.g. *go on, keep on, lead on, play on.* A light or a tap can be *on* or *off.*

In indicates collapse, as in *give in*: colloquial *done in* or *all in* (exhausted).

Off suggests departure, as in *set off* and *They're off* (i.e. have started, in a race). The departure may be very sudden, as in *The firework almost went off in my face.*

Out can suggest movement in any direction away from a starting point, as in *Set out* (= start), *Give out these papers* (i .e. hand one to everybody) and *The soldiers spread out* (i.e. moved away from one another). *Out* can also suggest disappearance, as in *Blow out the light. The fire is out. Burn out, die out.*

Up has three special meanings:

(a) it can serve as a means of arousing and encouraging, as in *hurry up!* (but *don't hurry*), *speak up* (i.e. speak more loudly, or don't be afraid to speak), *play up, keep up* (i.e. don't go slowly).

(b) it can indicate stoppage, as in *give up* (i.e. surrender), *hold up* (i.e. delay), *the game is up* (it's no use continuing the struggle).

Up (in its third special meaning) and *out* are also often used to emphasise the completion of the act. Notice the difference in the ways *eat* is used in the following examples:

[9]   Some people eat too much. (**SO**)

[10] Eat up your dinner! Finish it. (**I O**)

[11] You are eating too quickly. (**I U**)

[12] I am eating it all up. (**IU**)

We can imagine a mother saying [10] and [11] to a child, and the child replying with [12]. In *I eat* and *I am eating* we are concerned with the act as a whole, *I am eating* emphasising the action in progress. In *I eat up* and *I am eating up* we are concerned with the completion of the act, *eating up* emphasising the idea of being in the process of completing the act. Similarly, we have *I drink, I am drinking, I drink up, I am drinking up.*

Other examples of *up* used in this way are:

[13] We've saved up (money) to buy a house!

[14] Look up this word in the dictionary.

[15] Why not call up a few friends and ask them round for a party?

Save is also used without *up*, as in *Don't waste electricity. Save it!* *Up* could be omitted in example [13], but then the idea of having completed the saving would be lost. *Up* could not be omitted from examples [14] and [15].

Out is also used to indicate completion of the act as in

[16] I've found out what is wrong with this machine.

[17] May I point out where you have made a mistake?

[18] I can't solve this problem. How did you work it out?

Out could perhaps be omitted from example [16], but not from [17] and [18].

9.25 ADVERBIAL PARTICLE + PREPOSITION

It frequently happens, especially in spoken English, that direction and position are indicated by an adverbial particle (or even two particles) followed immediately by a preposition. Examples:

[19] We walked on (i.e. continued our journey) to Rome.

[20] I'm just going across over to the grocer's.

[21] I'll come along (the road) to the station with you.

[22] Go down to the kitchen.

[23] John's gone off to school.

[24] He's gone up to the senior school now.

[25] Can you help me get up onto the roof?

[26] Where's John?
        – He's up on the roof.

[27] We must have something in reserve to fall back on.

Note the difference between *on to*, in example [19], and *onto* and between *up on* in example [26] and *upon*.

9.26 PHRASAL VERBS

What are generally called 'phrasal verbs', i.e. constructions consisting of verbs plus the little words we have been discussing in this chapter, are very frequently used in English. In the main, these constructions are formed by the verb *be* or a simple verb expressing physical action – *come, go; put, take; give, get; do, make; let, keep; bring, send; stand, fall, sit; turn; break, tear, throw; walk, run, jump* – followed by a preposition or particle indicating direction or position.

The student should have no difficulty in understanding *Mr Smith is in, out, away, back. He has gone (or come) in, out, inside, outside, up, down. It's raining – put the chairs inside. It's stopped – take them out again. I've given away all my money. How can I get it back again? You'll have to do without. Please let me in – don't keep me out in the rain. Don't stop – keep on. I'll keep in front – you keep up with the rest of the party. Send my breakfast up to my room. Bring it back, I haven't finished. I'll send it round to your office. Stand up, stand outside. Don't fall down, don't fall over. Sit down, but sit up straight. Turn round, turn over. Thieves broke in. Fire broke out. Who's torn up my paper? Who's torn down the notice I put up on the board? Walk out quietly. The dish ran away with the spoon. Our dog ran along behind the car.*

These phrases tend to become fixed expressions with special meanings. Thus, in the morning *I wake up, get up* and *am* then *up* (i.e. out of bed). My bedroom is on the second floor: I am upstairs. I go downstairs, and am then *down. I put on* my hat and *go out.* The streets are crowded: I try to *get on* but am *held up* by the traffic. So *I make up* my mind to *go back* till the rush is *over.* That is simple enough, and the student can easily get into the habit of using such expressions. The meaning may not be so obvious, though it should now be understandable, in phrases like *Stand up to him, don't be afraid, fight back. I'll try, but don't feel up to it. I'll stand up for you, I won't let you down. I've given you my word and I won't go back on it. We'll see this through together. We won't give up the struggle: If there are difficulties, we'll put up with them.*

What are generally called 'phrasal verbs' are of four main types:

1. **Verb + preposition**, or prepositional verb (see Chapter 7). The meaning should by now be obvious in prepositional verbs like *laugh at, look for, talk about, write about.* The meaning is not so obvious in idiomatic phrasal verbs like *come across.* All constructions of this type are transitive, i.e. they must be followed by an object, and many of them can be put into the passive, as in *Have we dealt with this question before? Has it been dealt with already?* Note that the preposition, if monosyllabic, is unstressed, so that stress falls on the verb, not on the preposition, in *Has this been dealt with? What are you looking at?*

2. **Verb + adverbial particle**. There are innumerable combinations with *break, come, get, keep, stand, fall, run, turn, walk* and the particles mentioned in 9.23 and 9.24. The meaning of many of them, e.g. *come in*, needs no explanation: it is enough to say that in normal everyday English *come in* would occur more frequently than the more formal *enter*. The meaning of idiomatic phrasal verbs, like *give in* or *give up* is less obvious, though in those cases *in* and *up* are simply used as in 9.24. Constructions of this type are intransitive and do not occur in the passive. The particle is stressed.

3. **Verb + object + particle.** This meaning is obvious in *Take this rubbish away, Take away this rubbish, Take it away* and in innumerable other expressions in which *put, take, get, give, do, make, let, keep, bring, send, turn, break, tear, throw* etc., i.e. transitive verbs expressing physical action, especially monosyllabic ones, are combined with *away, back* and other particles referring to direction. The meaning is not obvious in idiomatic phrasal verbs such as *make up*, in the sense of 'invent' a story or '*turn down*', i.e. reject a proposal. Whether used literally or metaphorically, all constructions on this pattern are transitive and can be put into the passive. (*This rubbish must be taken away*.) The particle is, again, stressed.

4. **Verb + particle + prepositional + object**. Again, the particle is stressed, the preposition unstressed. The passive is sometimes found, as in the informal *This work must be got on with at once. This is not a situation that can be put up with easily.*

COMMENTARY AND DISCUSSION POINTS

Again, this chapter reflects Close's view that grammar consists of a spectrum varying from broad, generalisable principles or categories, to isolated uses which need to be learned. In this case his schema is clear:

Prepositions of place – both concrete and accessible

Prepositions of time – often understandable as extensions of the place concept

Relatively literal extensions of the space/time meanings

Metaphorical extensions of the space/time meanings

Truly 'exceptional' fixed phrases, which need to be learned by 'mechanical association'

Do you find this schema helpful for your own understanding? Do you think it can usefully be introduced to students as a pedagogic aid?

Students frequently see prepositions as wholly illogical, and an unending sea of isolated bits of information. What ways can you think of of helping to counteract the feeling of hopelessness that this can induce:

a.   in the way you **present** or **practise** prepositions?

b.   in the way you encourage students to **record** prepositions and prepositional phrases?

10   Adverbials

The main problem with adverbials—single-word adverbs (e.g. *badly, often*) or adverbial phrases (*to Spain*)—is to know where to put them. There are numerous kinds of adverbial, but they have one thing in common: they do not normally stand between the verb and its object. Nor do they occur between the object and the particle in a phrasal verb. Thus, *very well* and *strictly* are in their normal, proper positions in:

[1]   Eric speaks English very well.

[2]   They brought their children up strictly.

In *I don't like very much sugar*, *very much* is a quantifier meaning 'a great amount of'. In *I don't like sugar very much*, the same phrase is an adverbial making the sentence mean 'My liking for sugar is not very great.'

Exceptionally, an adverb may separate verb and object; but there must be a good reason for making the exception, e.g. to avoid ambiguity, or because the object is a long noun phrase, or to produce a dramatic effect. Thus in:

[3]   We must examine carefully the meanings of the words we use.

ambiguity would result if *carefully* were placed after *use* instead of after *examine*; and in:

[4]   He opened, very slowly, the most amazing book I have ever seen.

the delay in introducing the object creates an atmosphere of suspense.

Adverbials are of two main types: first, there are those that form part of the structure of a sentence, being usually pronounced within its main intonation pattern, and called adjuncts; second, there are those that fall outside the sentence structure, are pronounced before the main intonation pattern begins or after it ends, or interrupt the intonation: these occur normally in a sentence that follows another sentence, and for that reason they are called sentence adverbials. This second type can itself be sub-divided. There are disjuncts (e.g. *perhaps, personally*) which, like the modals in their secondary function, allow the speaker to express a personal attitude towards the statement (s)he is making; and conjuncts (e.g. *therefore, however*) which serve as logical links between one sentence or paragraph and another.

Occasionally, the same word may serve as adjunct in one sentence and disjunct in another. For example:

[5]   Nancy was not behaving naturally.

✗[6]   Naturally, I imagined she was feeling upset.

[7]   Peter did not behave properly.

[8]   Quite properly, he was punished for it.

In [5], *naturally* is an adjunct and the intonation pattern includes, and falls on, that word. In [6], *naturally (I imagined)* means 'it seemed to me natural': *naturally* has an intonation to itself, and is separated from the rest of the sentence by a comma. Similar comments could be made on *properly*. Example [6] could be re-arranged as follows:

✗ [6a] I imagined she was feeling upset, naturally.

or

✗ [6b] I imagined, naturally, she was feeling upset.

The commas in [6a] and [6b] are obligatory. The comma in [6a] marks the end of the main intonation pattern, while the commas in [6b] mark an interruption in the pattern. Similar comments would apply to the position of conjuncts and to the punctuation used with them.

The chief source of difficulty with adverbials is with adjuncts, which are of various kinds, as we shall see below. The most usual place for an adjunct is at the end of a sentence, after the obligatory elements in the sentence pattern. In the sentence *He makes watches*, all the elements SVO, are obligatory, and an adjunct like *beautifully* will come at the end, to produce SVO A. The element A is structurally optional there, providing additional information. Notice that the sentence *He makes watches beautifully* answers the question 'How does he make watches?' and that the emphasis in the answer falls on *beautifully*.

An adjunct can also occur in the middle of a sentence, as in

[9]   He slowly opened that amazing book.

There, the sentence answers the question 'What exactly did he do?': *slowly* does not add information at the end but, rather, modifies the verb. The mid-position adverb is thus intimately connected with the verb, is almost a part of it, as though there were a verb to *slowly-open*. Fear of the grammarian's taboo on the 'split infinitive' as it is called, caused me to insert a hyphen between slowly and open. Yet *I want you to creep downstairs and to slowly open the front door* might sound perfectly natural in spoken English, whereas **He used to beautifully make watches* would sound as alien as **He speaks very well Russian*.

This is relevant to single-word adverbs of frequency: *always, frequently, generally, never, occasionally, often, rarely, seldom, sometimes, usually* (and *ever* in questions and the negative). These adverbs are closely associated with verbal aspect (see Chapter 5), insofar as they draw attention to a series of acts. **S O** is exemplified in *I always go, I often go* etc.; and **S U** in *You're always tapping on the table*: indeed, *always* or *constantly*, is an essential factor in that particular example of **S U**. Similarly, single-word adverbs of degree (e.g. *almost, hardly, just*[1], *nearly, quite*[2], *scarcely*) that usually indicate the degree to which an act is completed and adverbs of relative time (*already, just, lately, recently, soon, still, yet*), which are obviously aspects of time, are closely associated with the verb and are usually found in the mid-position of the sentence.

The mid-position can be defined with reference to the operator (6.2), the adverb coming immediately after the operator, as in

[10] You are always tapping....I have often seen you doing it.

[11] He has never been seen again.

It will come immediately before a verb in the Simple Present or Simple Past (*I always go. He never went*); but if *do* as an operator is required, the mid-position adverb immediately follows it as before, as in

[12] I do sometimes take you out for dinner, you know.

In an emphatic affirmative, especially in contradiction to a negative, the adverb can precede the operator, which is then strongly stressed:

[13] You never go by bus these days.
    – I beg your pardon. I always do go by bus.

In answer to a question that requires a definite or emphatic statement of frequency, a normally mid-position adverb can come at the end of the sentence, as in

[14] How often do you go to see your dentist?
    – I don't know exactly, but I go sometimes.

Frequently, generally, occasionally, often could replace *sometimes* in that example; and we can say *I've been there recently* (or *lately*), *I haven't been there yet, I'll go soon*. But *just* and *never* would not be found in final position, nor would the single-word adverbs of degree already mentioned. Adverbs of frequency that can end a sentence can also come at the beginning, especially for contrast with something that has been said before: e.g.

[1] *Just* can be an adverb of degree, as in *I just passed my examination*, i.e. I obtained the minimum pass mark. It can also be an adverb of relative time, e.g. *I have just seen the results*, i.e. very recently. Or it can be a focusing adverb, as in *He just ran*, i.e. he did that and nothing else.

[2] *Quite* means 'moderately' before a 'gradable' adjective or adverb, e.g. *good, carefully*, but 'absolutely' before an 'ungradable' word, e.g. *right, perfectly*.

[15] I never miss my breakfast. Sometimes, it's true, I only have a piece of toast.

Never, like *hardly, scarcely, seldom* and *rarely* (indeed, like any other word implying a negative) could not begin a sentence without inversion of subject and verb:

[16] Never (Seldom, Rarely) has there been such a spectacle.

Compare this with *Only then did I realise how serious the situation was. Ever,* on the other hand, always occupies mid-position:

[17] Have you ever/Did you ever/Do you ever put your foot on a snake?

Still and *yet* at the beginning of a sentence are usually conjuncts, the former meaning 'All the same', the latter 'Nevertheless'.

In the interrogative like [17], the mid-position adverb follows operator + subject. In the negative, it usually follows operator +*not*:

[18] I haven't ever been there. We haven't often thought about it.

Nearly would fit into the pattern of [18] but *almost* would not occur with a negative. Nor would *never, hardly, rarely, seldom, scarcely,* since they are all negative in meaning, and a double negative is unacceptable in English. *Sometimes* normally comes before the operator + *not* (e.g. *I sometimes don't go to bed till twelve.*). *Still* can come before or after *not,* but with a difference in meaning; *He's not still working* means that he has stopped working, while *He's still not working* means that he has not started working yet.

Adverbs of manner typically come at the end of a sentence. However, what may appear to be adverbs of manner are not always easy to place. In examples [19] and [20], *legally* is an adverb of manner; and note that such an adverb can come before or after a passive construction. In example [21], the same word acts as a viewpoint adverb, and can occupy the same points as a disjunct or conjunct with the same effect on intonation and punctuation:

[19] We drew up the agreement legally.

[20] It was legally drawn up. (or drawn up legally)

[21] Legally (i.e. from a legal point of view), the agreement is perfectly in order.

There is a difference between these examples:

[22] (a) He kindly wrote to me.

    (b) He wrote to me kindly.

In [22] (a) the adverb is closely linked with the subject. Note a similar difference between [23] and [24]:

[23] I foolishly forgot to sign the letter.

[24] In doing so, I acted absent-mindedly rather than foolishly.

A subtler distinction is found in [25] and [26]:

⋇[25] I remember that incident well. I well remember it.

[26] You told that story well. But not *You well told it.

Well is an adverb of manner in [26], answering the question 'How did I tell that story?' Now an adverb of manner can modify a verb expressing action over which human control is possible, but not a verb of perception or cognition, like *see, hear, know, remember. Well* in [25] does not answer the question 'How do you remember that incident?' but 'How clearly do you remember it?'. *Well* in [25] is therefore an adverb of degree. A similar distinction is seen in these:

[27] I clearly remember the morning George came to school.

[28] He wrote all his notes very clearly.

Adverbs of time and position normally come at the end of the sentence. They can also be placed at the beginning, for emphasis, to set the scene in time or place, or for contrast with a previous statement. Adverbs of direction are usually found only at the end. However, if place (position or direction) and time occur in the same sentence, place normally precedes time. In both, place and time, more precise details are given before more general information. Thus:

[29] Columbus reached America in the late fifteenth century.

[30] He landed on the 12th of October 1492.

[31] Early in 1493, he returned to Spain (but not *To Spain he returned early in 1493).

[32] He died at Valladolid in Spain in May 1506.

[33] Throughout Latin America, October 12th is an annual holiday.

Only (meaning 'that and nothing else'), *even* (meaning 'that in addition to everything else') and *also* (meaning 'in addition to what has been mentioned already'), all focus attention on one particular element in a sentence. Uncertainty may arise, at least in writing, if the adverb is not placed as closely as possible to the element on which attention is meant to be focused. This uncertainty is less likely in spoken English, where the element concerned can be pronounced with stress and on a higher pitch than the rest of the sentence. Thus, though the speaker's precise meaning in *We can only lend these books to members of the library* may be conveyed quite clearly in speech, in print that sentence focuses attention on *lend* (and might suggest, for example, that the books cannot be sold). *Only these books* would highlight *these books*, while *only* after *library* would highlight *members of the library*. Similar comments would apply to *even* and *also*.

Very is an intensifier and can modify adjectives and adverbs provided they are gradable: thus *very good, very carefully* but not **very unique, *very perfectly*. *Very* can be used with certain participal adjectives, i.e. *-ing* and *-ed* forms, e.g. *very interesting, very tired*. But only those *-ing* and *-ed* forms that have been fully established as adjectives can safely be modified by *very*; and in many cases other intensifiers must be used. Note that *highly* tends to be used with words suggesting a good quality, while *utterly* frequently occurs with words suggesting the reverse, as in *utterly boring*. *Deeply* is often used with participal adjectives referring to feelings and emotions, as in *deeply disappointed, deeply hurt;* but *badly* or *seriously hurt* physically. Other examples are *completely forgotten, fully insured, thoroughly worn out* and *widely known*.

COMMENTARY AND DISCUSSION POINTS

In most grammar books the adverb section is a notorious dustbin section, in which all the words that will not fit anywhere else are placed. Many modern grammarians separate intensifiers from other adverbs.

Perhaps the most important point Close makes is that the key problem with adverbs is their position in the sentence, and the fact that different kinds of adverbs have a different range of possible positions. Unfortunately, classroom teaching about adverbs is often reduced to the morphological rule *adverb = adjective + -ly*.

Which kinds of adverbs do you think are most useful to a foreign learner?

What about adverbial phrases rather than one word adverbs?

Can you think of another example similar to the distinction between *She is still not working* and *She is not still working*?

Can you make a list of sentence adverbs and adverbials (*Frankly, To be honest ...*) which:
   a.   You think **you use** frequently yourself in speech?
   b.   Which you think would be **useful to students**?

As this is the last chapter, it provides an opportunity to invite the reader to think back over the other chapters of the book – can you recall generalisations which the author has drawn to your attention which seem to you to be particularly powerful? In what ways has your understanding of the regular structure of the English verb been affected? How many of the Primary Distinctions of chapter 2 come to mind?

Perhaps most important of all, can you list ways in which what you have read in this book has changed your own understanding of grammar, and/or the way you present, explain or practise things in the classroom?

INDEX

1. Individual words dealt with from a grammatical point of view are printed in italic. Grammatical terms and notions are in ordinary type.
2. adj. = adjective; adv. = adverb; det. = determiner; part. = particle; prep. = preposition; v 'in contrast with'.

Further reading

If you have enjoyed *A Teachers' Grammar* and found it useful you may be interested in some other LTP publications:

IF YOU WANT TO KNOW MORE ABOUT GRAMMAR:

The English Verb, Michael Lewis, 0 906717 40 X, LTP 1986.
A step by step survey of the central problem of English — the structure of the verb. Extensive discussion of the grammar itself, and of classroom rules. Practical hints on how to present grammar in the classroom. Recommended reading on RSA and other book lists.

Grammar and Practice, Jimmie Hill et al 0 906717 74 4, LTP, 1989.
Classroom explanations at two levels, and extensive and varied practice material. A clear distinction between form and meaning; grammar explanations and practices which explore meaning. Many powerful and effective practices, way beyond mechanical transformations and fill-in exercises.

IF YOU WANT TO KNOW MORE ABOUT LANGUAGE TEACHING:

The Lexical Approach, Michael Lewis, 0 906717 99 X, LTP 1993.
Subtitled *The State of ELT and a Way Forward*, this book provides a comprehensive evaluation of the theory and practice of current ELT. Discussion of the grammar/vocabulary dichotomy and a clear statement of the implications of taking a lexical view of language. Innovative and challenging, it is ideal for teachers with some classroom experience and training.